THE HOLMAN BIBLE ATLAS
INCLUDING
THE LAND AND PEOPLE
OF THE BIBLE

THE HOLMAN

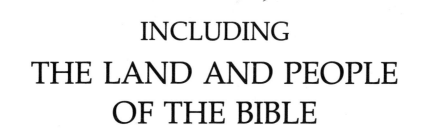

INCLUDING
THE LAND AND PEOPLE
OF THE BIBLE

Edited by
JERRY L. HOOPER

A.J. HOLMAN COMPANY
Division of J. B. Lippincott Company
Philadelphia and New York

U. S. Library of Congress Cataloging in Publication Data

Jerry L. Hooper
The Holman Bible atlas

Includes indexes
I. Bible—Geography—Maps. 1. Hooper,
Jerry L. II. Title: Bible atlas.
G2230.H64   1978   912'.1'22   78-12606
ISBN-0-87981-099-8

Credits:
Greek Vase, Vatican Museum, Rome
Copper Adzes, Department of Antiquities, Jerusalem
Oumran Scroll, Hekhal Hasefer, Jerusalem
Hornblower, Hittite Museum, Ankara
Egyptian Scroll, British Museum, London
Maps by: William Stanke, Kyo Takahashi

All Scripture Quotations are from the
New American Standard Bible
and are used by permission of
The Lockman Foundation.

The relative scale map: copyright 1944 by NATIONAL PUBLISHING COMPANY.
Used by permission.

CONTENTS

THE ATLAS

THE LAND AND PEOPLE OF THE BIBLE

INTRODUCTION

The Atlas

ANYONE who studies the Bible, teaches Bible classes, plans a trip to the Holy Land (or would like to) will find this atlas an indispensable tool to use over and over again.

The thirty-eight maps show the terrain of biblical lands and trace major biblical events. (See the list of maps on page 109 .)

An index of all sites plotted on these maps is on page 84 .

Colorful illustrations, each with a caption, accompany the maps, describe the biblical, historical, and archaeological significance of what is pictured. Wherever the subject of an illustration is directly relevant to a biblical passage, that passage is included.

An index of all illustrations is on page 107.

An index of all scripture quotations is on page 111 .

The Land and People of The Bible

A survey of the major geographical areas, the history, geology, topography, climate, vegetation, animals, minerals and the people who have inhabited this land from the beginning is included. The moving story of this land and people is explored from the pre-Israelite era through the New Testament age. Scenes of the actual geographical and historical sites help to make this truly an armchair tour of the Holy Land and a valuable aid to biblical understanding.

An index of all illustrations is on page 107 .

An index of all scripture quotations is on page 111.

Bible Atlas

MT. ARARAT

The mountainous region of Ararat is approximately midway between the Black and the Caspian seas. Mount Ararat is a name associated with the double-peaked mountain in the background of this photograph. The higher peak is nearly 17,000 feet above sea level.

And in the seventh month, on the seventeenth day of the month, the ark rested upon the mountains of Ararat.

GENESIS 8:4

And the Lord God planted a garden toward the east, in Eden. . . .

Now a river flowed out of Eden to water the garden; and from there it divided and became four rivers.

And the name of the third river is Tigris; it flows east of Assyria. And the fourth river is the Euphrates.

GENESIS 2:8, 10, 14

A river flowed out of Eden and became four main branches, two of which are known with certainty: the Tigris, called Hiddekel in the Bible, and the Euphrates. The map shows the present course of these two rivers. What is today called the Near East is in the center of this map and is bounded roughly by five bodies of water: the Mediterranean Sea, the Black Sea, the Caspian Sea, the Persian Gulf, and the Red Sea. Parentheses around these and certain other names on this map indicate names that through the centuries came to be used for these geographic features. Though generally barren—with mountains, hills, and deserts—the Near East contains a well-watered region from which arose the first great civilizations of the world. Because of its abundant vegetation and its shape, this region has been called the Fertile Crescent; it extends from the Persian Gulf, which is the mouth of the Tigris and Euphrates rivers, northwestward before curving south along the coast of the Mediterranean Sea toward the Nile Delta. A map of the Fertile Crescent, tracing the route of Abraham on his journey to Canaan, is on page 15. In the mountains of Ararat (see map) Noah's ark came to rest after the Flood.

SEAT OF CIVILIZATION

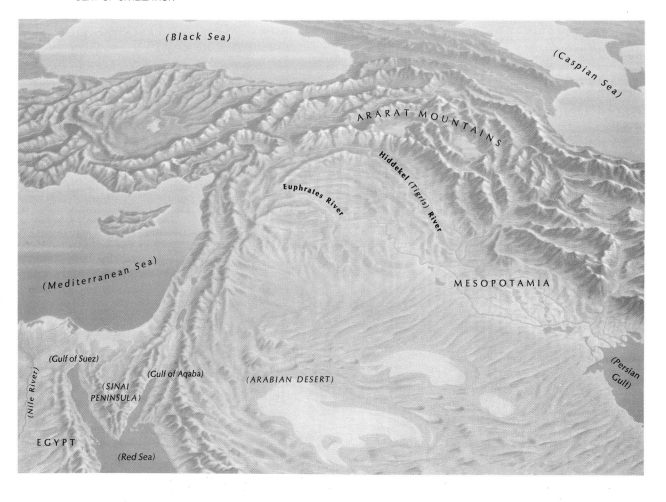

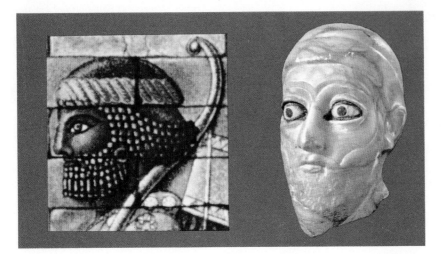

Shem, "the father of all the children of Eber" (Gen. 10:21), was the ancestor of the Hebrews. Here we see how he and some of his descendants may have looked (left to right); the lands they lived in are indicated on the map on

page 13. Elam—a people that lived to the east of Babylonia. The picture shows the archers in the palace of Susa (5th century B.C.). Shem—the head is that of an East Semitic ruler of the city of Adab (from the end of the third millennium [about 2000] B.C.). Eber—the people to which the children of Israel belonged and which included West and South Semitic tribes. The reproduction depicts an inhabitant from the patriarchal period (18th century B.C.). Aram—a people that, at the end of the second millennium [about 1000] B.C., spread as far as Syria and Palestine. The relief is from Zinjirli and portrays the Armean king Bar-Rakab of the 8th century B.C. Asshur—one of the great peoples of Mesopotamia, which reached its apogee in the 8th and 7th centuries B.C. The picture shows the head of an Assyrian on a relief of this period. Joktan is usually regarded as the father of the South Arabian tribes.

DESCENDANTS OF SHEM

The sons of Shem were Elam and Asshur and Arpachshad and Lud and Aram.

And Arpachshad became the father of Shelah; and Shelah became the father of Eber.

And two sons were born to Eber; the name of one was Peleg, for in his days the earth was divided; and his brother's name was Joktan.

GENESIS 10:22, 24–25

Chapters 10 through 12 of Genesis list the descendants of Noah and certain of the territories in which they settled—a Biblical "table of nations." Plotted on this map are the areas that the descendants of Japheth, Ham, and Shem—the sons of Noah—probably inhabited, as indicated by archaeological evidence.

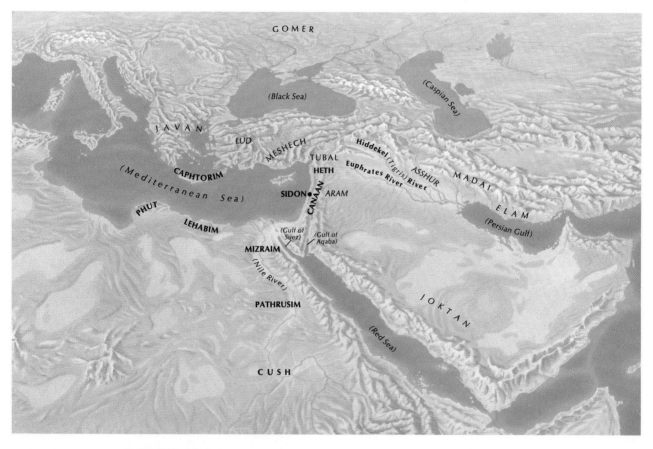

TABLE OF NATIONS

From these the coastlands of the nations were separated into their lands, every one according to his language, according to their families, into their nations.

GENESIS 10:5

SPRING IN THE DESERT OF SOUTHERN NEGEB

Now the angel of the Lord found her by a spring of water in the wilderness, by the spring on the way to Shur.　Genesis 16:7

Wandering in the desert, Hagar came upon a spring of water. In the almost waterless Negeb, such oases form natural resting-places for wayfarers. Indeed, the very existence of the nomads depends on the springs which supply them with water for their flocks and serve as camping-places on the desert tracks. In her flight, Hagar followed one of the tracks leading to her native Egypt, the way to Shur, which is mentioned again in the story of the Exodus.

The picture shows a spring and palms in the desert of the southern Negeb.

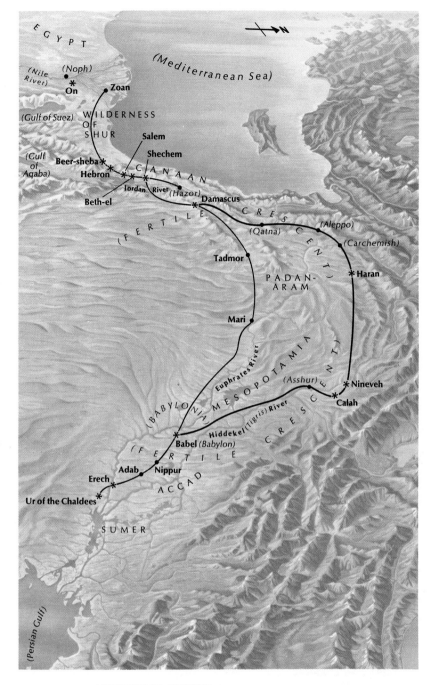

The migration of Abram and his family from Ur of the Chaldees, by way of Haran, to Canaan (GEN. 11:31; 12:1–9) and later into Egypt (GEN. 12:10) presumably followed caravan routes which linked centers of population. These places, from Mesopotamia to Egypt, are known to us today from routes described on 18th century B.C. clay tablets discovered at Mari and from itineraries of travelers on tablets unearthed at numerous other sites. These centers of early civilization and the routes linking them are shown on this map. Abram's migration, following the northern route through Haran, is indicated by the heavier line. Cities mentioned in the Book of Genesis are plotted with asterisks.

MIGRATION OF ABRAHAM

Now the Lord said to Abram,
   "Go forth from your country,
   And from your relatives
And from your father's house,
To the land which I will show you

GENESIS 12:1

15

LANDSCAPE IN NORTHERN SINAI

Then Moses led Israel from the Red Sea, and they went out into the wilderness of Shur; and they went three days in the wilderness and found no water.

EXODUS 15:22

After the Israelites had crossed the "Sea of Suf" (in the English Bible translated "the Red Sea"), they turned toward the desert wastes of the Sinai peninsula. That closest to the Egyptian border was the biblical wilderness of Shur, which apparently stretched from "the way of the land of the Philistines" and Lake Serbonis southward to the Tih plateau in Central Sinai. The word "shur" in Hebrew means "wall," and maybe it designated the line of forts erected by the Egyptians on their desert frontier, from Migdol near the Mediterranean coast in the north to the Gulf of Suez in the south (i.e., along the modern Suez Canal). The forts were intended to defend the soil of Egypt from Asiatic desert raiders and to control their movements into the land of the Nile.

By their daring march along the sea, the Israelites had outflanked the northern end of this fortified line and then continued southeast until they came to a waterless waste "in the way of Shur."

The picture shows a sandy and rocky desert landscape in Northern Sinai.

16

THE EXODUS: EGYPT TO SINAI

When the firstborn son in every Egyptian family died in fulfillment of Moses' prophecy (Ex. 11–12), the Pharaoh allowed the Israelites to leave Egypt (Ex. 12:31). Gathering at the city of Raamses, they set out for Canaan. When they reached the northwestern edge of the Sinai desert, the Lord commanded them to camp between the Great Sea (the Mediterranean) and a network of Egyptian forts barring the way along the coast. From the area of Migdol, God guided the Israelites southward, away from the land of the Philistines (Ex. 13:17) across the Sea of Reeds (usually translated "the Red Sea"), and through the desert to Mount Sinai. The route shown is based largely on the one traditionally inferred from the Scriptures.

*T*ell the sons of Israel to turn back and camp before Pi-hahiroth, between Migdol and the sea; you shall camp in front of Baal-zephon, opposite it, by the sea.

EXODUS 14:2

The Israelites' main base during the long years of wandering was the fertile valley of Kadesh. Miriam, Moses' sister, died here (NUM. 20:1). Kadesh was the most important oasis on the northern fringe of the Sinai desert, and capable of supporting a large encamped host. Remains from every period of biblical history have been found at Kadesh; in the foreground are ruined walls of a fortress built by Jehoshaphat (873–849 B.C.) or Uzziah (783–742 B.C.), kings of Judah, to protect the southern border of the land.

VALLEY OF KADESH

So you remained in Kadesh many days, the days that you spent there.

DEUTERONOMY 1:46

The Book of Numbers begins with Moses organizing—"numbering"—the Israelites into tribes, and ends as they approach Jericho, the first Canaanite city they would attack after crossing the Jordan (JOSH. 2–6). This map traces their major routes from Mount Sinai to Canaan, completing the journey from Egypt that began in the Book of Exodus (13–40). At some point, Kadesh-Barnea apparently became their main base (NUM. 20). Shortly after the Israelites moved north from Kadesh-Barnea, the high priest Aaron, brother of Moses, died on Mount Hor (NUM. 20:28). In the last phase of their journey, the Israelites marched along the eastern edge of Edom and Moab and, north of Moab, along the King's Highway (NUM. 20:17; 21:12–22). In the battle of Jahaz the Israelites defeated the Amorites. Finally, the children of God turned eastward toward Canaan, avoiding the fortresses of the land of the Ammonites (DEUT. 2:19). These fortresses are plotted on the map on the basis of archaeological investigations. At Mount Nebo, overlooking the Promised Land, Moses died (DEUT. 34:1–5).

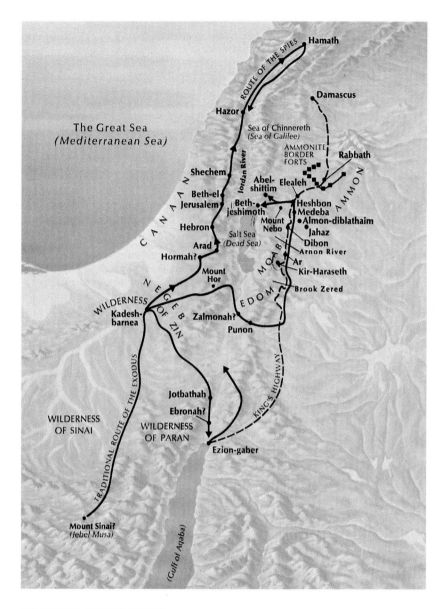

THE EXODUS: SINAI TO CANAAN

Now these are the records of the generations of Aaron and Moses at the time when the Lord spoke with Moses on Mount Sinai.

NUMBERS 3:1

Then Joshua turned back at that time, and captured Hazor and struck its king with the sword; for Hazor formerly was the head of all these kingdoms. Joshua 11:10

The commanding position of Hazor at the junction of several international trade routes gave it great strategic importance and made it the most powerful of the Canaanite cities of the north. Hence the biblical description of it as "the head of all those kingdoms." From cuneiform documents it is clear that, as early as the first third of the second millennium B.C., Hazor had become a famous commercial center and that its renown had spread as far as Mari in Mesopotamia. Egyptian records and the el-Amarna Letters indicate that in the second half of the second millennium B.C. Hazor was the center of an important kingdom which had extended its way as far as the region of Ashtaroth in Bashan. In the time of the Israelite Kingdom it was once more an important fortified center (1 Kin. 9:15) and remained as such until the destruction of the cities of Galilee by Tiglath-pileser III.

The tell of Hazor, Tell el-Qadah (see the illustration), is one of the largest and most imposing in the Middle East. The citadel rises 120 feet above its surroundings and covers 25 acres. At its foot lay the lower town, which covered an area 3,000 feet long by 2,100 feet wide. This city was protected by a wall and earth-rampart built in the first half of the second millennium B.C. The excavations on the site have shown that the lower city flourished in the Canaanite period only, while the Israelite settlement was confined to the tell itself. The defeat of Jabin, king of Hazor, sealed the fate of the Canaanites in the north of the country.

THE TEL OF HAZOR

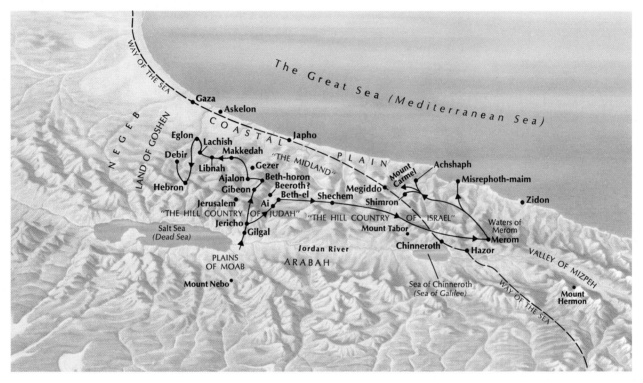

CONQUEST OF CANAAN

Thus Joshua took all that land: the hill country and all the Negev, all that land of Goshen, the lowland, the Arabah, the hill country of Israel and its lowland.

JOSHUA 11:16

The map shows the route of the Israelites in the Conquest of Canaan. The view is westward in the line of their advance on Jericho from the plains of Moab. From his base at Gilgal, Joshua moved into the country around Bethel. His main engagements were fought in hill country: at Ai, then Aijalon, and southward through the foothills to Lachish and Debir; and in the north, at the Waters of Merom near the Sea of Chinnereth. At the end of the fighting the following districts had fallen to the Israelites: (1) "the hill country of Judah"; (2) the Negeb—the southern desert of Judah; (3) the land of Goshen—the region south of Hebron where the city of Goshen was (see JOSH. 10:41; 15:51); (4) "the midland" (Shephelah)—the region of the lower slopes of the Judean mountains along the edge of the coastal plain; (5) the Arabah—the Jordan Valley; and (6) "the hill country of Israel," a term for the mountains of Ephraim and Galilee.

THE TERRITORY OF ISSACHAR

The fourth lot fell to Issachar, to the sons of Issachar according to their families.

And their territory was to Jezreel and included Chesulloth and Shunem.

JOSHUA 19:17–18

*The tribe of Issachar occupied the south, and particularly the southeast, of Lower Galilee. To the north it had a common border with Naphtali in the Valley of Yabneel and Mount Tabor, the latter being also one of the border-points of Zebulun. Included, too, in Issachar was the eastern part of the Valley of Jezreel; and the eastern border of the tribe apparently ran along the River Jordan. The southern border was constantly shifting. Beth-Shan and the region around it were allotted to the tribe of Manasseh, which made inroads into the territory of Issachar (*JOSH. *17:11; see map on p. 23. Issachar did not succeed in driving out the Canaanite inhabitants of the valley and actually became tributary to them, as is implied in the Blessing of Jacob: "Issachar is a strong donkey, lying down between the sheepfolds; . . .he bowed his shoulder to bear burdens, and became a slave at forced labor" (*GEN. *49:14–15).*

The territory of Issachar was partly flat and partly hilly. It contained two valleys, that of Jezreel to the south, and to the north that of Chesulloth, pictured here with the hill of Moreh (1,550 feet) in the background. The photograph was taken from the mountains of Nazareth looking south.

Thus the sons of Israel did just as the Lord had commanded Moses, and they divided the land.

JOSHUA 14:5

DIVISION OF CANAAN

Joshua allocated the land west of the Jordan among the nine and one-half remaining tribes; two and one-half of the twelve tribes had already received from Moses their portions on the eastern side of the river (DEUT. 33). The whole land was divided by lot among the different tribes, and most of them soon established themselves in part of their territories (JOSH. 17–18; JUDG. 1:27–36). Joshua 13 describes "the land that remains": the Philistine kingdom with its five principal cities; the whole of "the land of the Canaanite"—the coastal plain—from Gezer in the south to the Valley of Accho in the north; and the Valley of Jezreel. Also listed there are the northern districts of Canaan, most of which were outside the limits of the Israelite occupation: the Phoenician coastal cities; the land of the Gebalites, which stretched from the Lebanon range to Gebal on the Phoenician coast; and the eastern end of the Lebanon plain "from Baal-gad below Mount Hermon as far as Hamath (Lebo-hamath)." Moab and Edom in southern Transjordan also remained unconquered.

23

THE RIVER KISHON

The river Kishon flows through the Valley of Jezreel (see the map on p. 25) in a meandering course. During the greater part of the year only the western part of its course has a permanent flow. This part of the river (photographed here) runs along the foot of Mount Carmel and carries water that comes down from the northern slopes of Mount Ephraim and from Lower Galilee. In the rainy season the waters of the river rise, and in a particularly wet year they rush along in a turbulent current that sweeps away everything in its path. These features of the river are brought out in the Song of Deborah, which presumably describes its flooding in the rainy season, to the accompaniment of thunder and lightning. The flood took Sisera by surprise and swept away his chariots. The victory of the Israelites over Sisera's host was thus not entirely due to force of arms, but to the assistance of nature. Deborah saw in this a miracle: "The stars fought from heaven, from their courses they fought against Sisera" (JUDG. 5:20).

The torrent of Kishon swept them away,
The ancient torrent, the torrent Kishon.

JUDGES 5:21

24

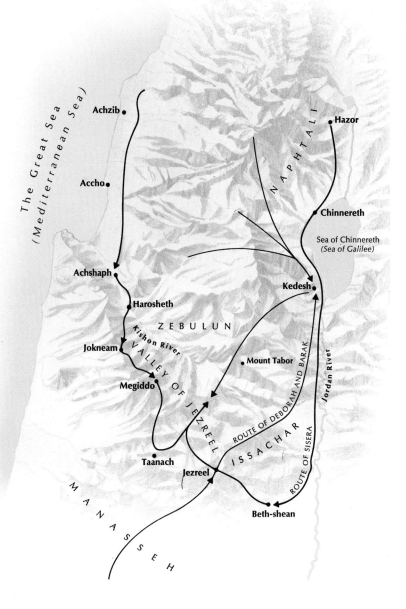

The prophetess Deborah was judge of Israel when King Jabin of Hazor was oppressing the northern tribes of Israel. With Deborah guiding him, Barak, an Israelite chieftain, made war against the armies of Jabin, which were commanded by Sisera. Barak gathered his army at Kedesh-Naphtali and moved on, for strategic reasons, to Mount Tabor. The Canaanites under Sisera had come down the shore of the Sea of Chinnereth, while the allied northern kings had moved south along the coast. The two Canaanite forces met between Megiddo and Jezreel and advanced northward. The Israelites defeated them on the plain beside Mount Tabor.

BATTLE OF BARAK AGAINST
JABIN AND SISERA, 195

And the Lord sold them into the hand of Jabin king of Canaan, who reigned in Hazor; and the commander of his army was Sisera, who lived in Harosheth-hagoyim.

And the sons of Israel cried to the Lord; for he had nine hundred iron chariots, and he oppressed the sons of Israel severely for twenty years.

JUDGES 4:2–3

And the ark of God was taken.   I Samuel 4:11

MIGDAL APHEK

The battle of Ebenezer (approximately in the middle of the 11th century B.C.) was fought by the Israelite tribes in an attempt to check the expansion of the Philistines into the central mountains of Palestine. The enemy had successfully forced their way along the coastal plain and into the mountains of Judah, and had gained the approaches to the mountains of Ephraim. The Philistine army was drawn up for battle at Aphek, which was situated on the northeastern edge of the area controlled by them. The site of Aphek is to be found in the large mound of Rosh ha-Ayin (in Arabic Ras el-Ein), at the source of the Yarkon. The Israelites, for their part, encamped by Ebenezer, the exact site of which has not been located. It must have been opposite Aphek in the foothills of Ephraim, near the modern Migdal Aphek (see the map). The battle resulted in a decisive victory for the Philistines, who captured the Ark of the Covenant from the Israelites (I Sam. 4:11). This victory gave the Philistines free access to the mountains of Ephraim, so that they were able to conquer the key places of the region, among them, apparently, Shiloh itself. Their control of this region lasted until the time of Saul.

Seen in the photograph here is the site of Migdal Aphek (Arabic Majdal Yaba), standing on a hill dominating the Shiloh Valley (Wadi Deir Ballut), which runs to the south of it. In the foreground is the level expanse of the Aphek gap, assumed to have been the scene of the battle against the Philistines.

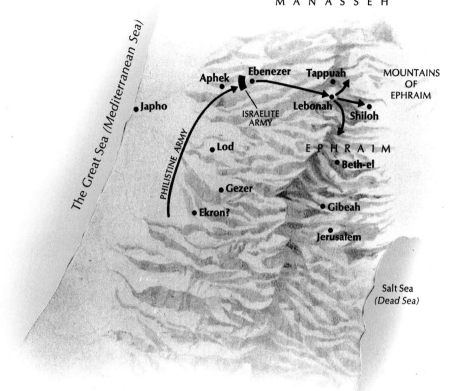

Thus the word of Samuel came to all Israel. Now Israel went out to meet the Philistines in battle and camped beside Ebenezer while the Philistines camped in Aphek.

I SAMUEL 4:1

At the fiercely fought battle of Ebenezer (about 1050 B.C.) the tribes of Israel attempted to check the expansion of the Philistines from the coastal plain into the central mountains of Ephraim and Manasseh. The result was a shattering defeat for the Israelites. They were beaten militarily and thousands of their warriors slain (I SAM. 4:2). In addition, the Philistines captured the Ark of the Covenant, which had been brought to the battlefield from the sanctuary at Shiloh in a desperate move to help the Israelite cause (I SAM. 4:4,11).

TEL MICHMASH

The primary task for which Saul was chosen king was to fight the Philistines. After the battle of Ebenezer and the destruction of Shiloh, the Philistines had penetrated deeply into the heart of the Israelite territory up to the main centers of Judah, Benjamin, and Ephraim. To check their advance, Saul disposed his forces at three key points in the mountains: at Bethel and Michmash under his own command, and at Gibeah of Benjamin under the command of Jonathan, his son (1 Sam. 13:2). Jonathan attacked first and succeeded in routing the Philistine garrison at Gibeah. The Philistines reacted by sending out a punitive expedition ("the raiders") against the center of the Israelite battle line at Michmash, while Saul with six hundred of his men entrenched himself at Gibeah of Benjamin (1 Sam. 13:15). The Philistines split their forces into three columns, which advanced north, west, and east. Now was the moment for Saul to act. After Jonathan's daring sally, he suddenly fell upon and defeated the main body of the Philistines, which was still at Michmash and consisted partly of Hebrew mercenaries. After Saul's victory, many of these mercenaries came over to his side (1 Sam. 14:21) and joined his troops in the pursuit of the Philistines, who fled westward past Aijalon (1 Sam. 14:31). The course of the battle is marked on the map.

The view above is of Tell Michmash, near modern Mukhmas, about seven miles northeast of Jerusalem.

Then Samuel arose and went up from Gilgal to Gibeah of Benjamin. And Saul numbered the people who were present with him, about six hundred men.

1 Samuel 13:15

28

BATTLE OF SAUL AND JONATHAN
AGAINST THE PHILISTINES

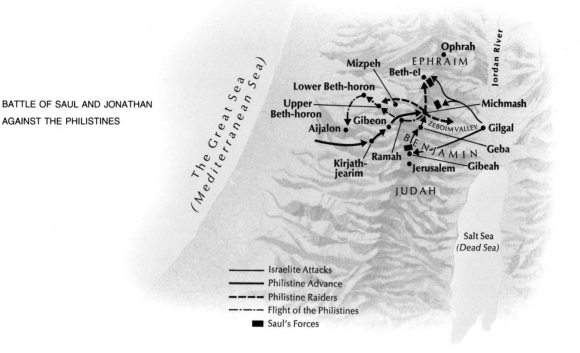

Israelite Attacks
Philistine Advance
Philistine Raiders
Flight of the Philistines
■ Saul's Forces

The Philistines had followed up their victory at Ebenezer and Shiloh by penetrating far into the Israelite territories of Judah, Benjamin, and Ephraim. King Saul countered by deploying his forces at three key points in the mountains—at Bethel, Michmash, and Gibeah of Benjamin. The major engagement occurred at Michmash (see map), where Saul defeated the main Philistine army and sent it fleeing westward past Aijalon (1 SAM. 14:31).

*N*ow Saul and his son Jonathan and the people who were present with them were staying in Geba of Benjamin while the Philistines camped at Michmash.

1 SAMUEL 13:16

REGION OF ADULLAM

So David departed from there and escaped to the cave of Adullam. I Samuel 22:1

After the fugitive David had failed to find refuge in the country of the Philistines (I Sam. 21:14-15), he made a hideout for himself at Adullam in the border country between Philistia and Judah. There he gathered around him a band of four hundred men (I Sam. 22:2) who made audacious sorties from this base into the surrounding district (II Sam. 23:13 ff.). Adullam, close to which lay David's cave, is located by most scholars at Tell esh-Sheikh Madkur in the Shephelah between the hills that dominate the Valley of Elah, at a height of 1,150 feet above sea level. The ancient name of the place is preserved in the nearby Khirbet Id

el-Ma. Adullam is mentioned as one of the thirty-one royal cities conquered by Joshua (Josh. 12:15) and was incorporated in the territory of Judah together with Socoh and Azekah (Josh. 15:35). Adullam had several natural advantages. Its position in the hills made it difficult of access and therefore a good place of refuge. Together with the neighboring settlements, the district contained rich agricultural soil, with fields for crop-growing in the valley and expanses of pasture on the lower slopes of the hills. Finally, the rocky terrain of Adullam was naturally suited to the digging of cisterns and the sinking of wells.

The region of Adullam is rich in mounds and ruins which show that it was densely populated in ancient times. The city itself was fortified in the reign of Rehoboam, King of Judah, to protect the road to Beth-Zur. Part of the rugged and broken region, with its hills and caves, is shown in the view above.

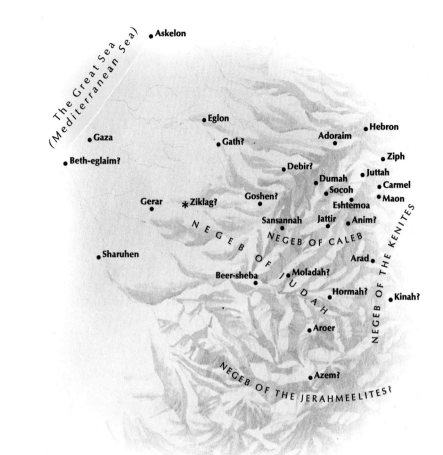

DAVID'S RAIDS IN THE NEGEV

Now Achish said, "Where have you made a raid today?" And David said, "Against the Negev of Judah and against the Negev of the Jerahmeelites and against the Negev of the Kenites."

I SAMUEL 27:10

Achish, the king of Gath, gave David a residence in the fortified city of Ziklag (1 SAM. 27:5–6). From this base, David made sorties into the Negeb desert against the Amalekite nomads who were constantly harassing the Israelite settlers. However, as a refugee in Philistia, David was compelled to mislead Achish by telling him that the targets of his sorties were parts of the Judean Negeb identified by the names of the Israelite clans and tribes that lived in them at the time of the Conquest of Canaan (1 SAM. 27:10); this suggests the area was sparsely settled and without established communities. Archaeological survey has indeed revealed that most of the towns in the Judean Negeb were founded a century or more after David.

And the lords of the Philistines were proceeding on by hundreds and by thousands, and David and his men were proceeding on in the rear with Achish. I Samuel 29:2

MT. GILBOA AND SPRING AREA NORTH OF JEZREEL

The battle against the Philistines, in which Saul and his sons met their death, was fought in the Valley of Jezreel, where the Philistine army had advanced from its forward base at Aphek, the modern Rosh ha-Ayin. The Valley of Jezreel was the scene of frequent fighting in antiquity, from the campaign of Thutmose III down to Deborah's battle against Jabin, King of Hazor, and Gideon's assault on the Midianites. Like the Canaanites before them, the Philistines undoubtedly chose this terrain because it allowed full use of their heavy equipment, and also because there they had strongly fortified cities (such as Beth-Shan) to serve as bases. The lightly armed Israelites, for their part, preferred to fight in the hills. By this battle, the Philistines tried to cut off the territory of the Joseph tribes from Galilee and to follow up their victory by an assault on the mountains of Ephraim by way of Beth-Hagan and the Valley of Dothan. They were not fighting to capture any particular place, but were intent on conquering the whole region traversed by the "Way of the Sea." Saul's troops encamped at the spring north of the city of Jezreel (see the view above) with their back toward this town and the steep Mount Gilboa. The battle ended in the utter defeat of the Israelites. The Philistines thereby regained control of considerable areas of Canaan which they had lost during Saul's reign. Saul's son Ishbaal (or Ishbosheth) and his commander-in-chief, Abner, the son of Ner, fled to Mahanaim in Transjordan, which they made their new capital.

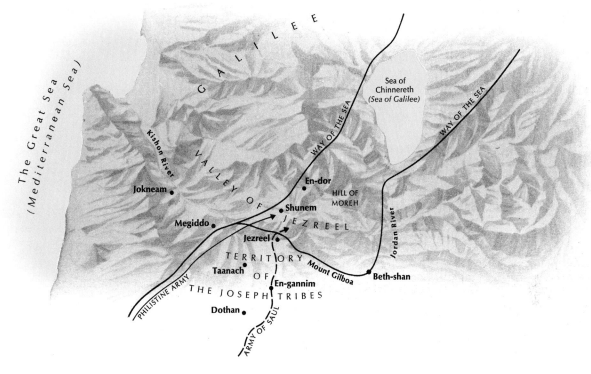

BATTLE IN THE VALLEY OF JEZREEL

*N*ow the Philistines gathered together all their armies to Aphek, while the Israelites were camping by the spring which is in Jezreel.

I SAMUEL 29:1

The battle against the Philistines in which Saul and his sons met their death was fought in the Valley of Jezreel, to where the Philistine army had advanced from its forward base at Aphek, the modern Rosh ha Ayin. The Valley of Jezreel was the scene of frequent fighting in antiquity, from the campaign of Thutmose III down to Deborah's battle against Jabin, king of Hazor, and Gideon's assault on the Midianites. Like the Canaanites before them, the Philistines undoubtedly chose this terrain because it allowed full use of their heavy equipment, and also because there they had strongly fortified cities (such as Beth-Shan) to serve as bases. The lightly armed Israelites, for their part, preferred to fight in the hills.

THE HOLY CITY

Praise of the Holy City and its Temple is a recurrent theme of the Psalms (see Ps. 78:68–69; 84; 93:5; 96:6). Such hymns may have been sung by caravans of pilgrims wending their way to the Temple, or in thanksgiving processions around the city wall. The prophets, in their ecstatic praise of Jerusalem, occasionally employ the characteristic imagery of the Psalms (Is. 26:1–2; JER. 17:12; 31:23). Zion, "the city of our God," is both holy and eternal in the Psalms. It is depicted as a mighty citadel that God will establish for ever (Ps. 48:8) and against whose towers every hostile onslaught will be shattered. The city is also "the perfection of beauty" (Ps. 50:2), "the joy of the whole earth" (LAM. 2:15); its palaces and towers are the wonder of all who behold them (Ps. 48:12–13). A similar theme is expressed in the verses above. Shown here is a view of Jerusalem from the east, with the site of the Temple mount, now marked by a mosque, at the far right.

Great is the Lord, and greatly to be praised, In the city of our God, His holy mountain....the joy of the whole earth, Is Mount Zion in the far north, The city of the great King.

PSALM 48:1–2

34

'Thus says the Lord, "Are you the one who should build Me a house to dwell in?

"For I have not dwelt in a house since the day I brought up the sons of Israel from Egypt, even to this day; but I have been moving about in a tent, even in a tabernacle."

II SAMUEL 7:5–6

The Ark of the Covenant, one of the most venerated of Israelite sacred objects because it housed the presence of God when he spoke to his people, was made during the Exodus (Ex. 25:10–22). After the Conquest of Canaan, the children of Israel placed the Ark—probably in a tabernacle-like dwelling—at Shiloh (Josh. 18:1). In this House of God, Samuel was priest. David himself pitched the tent that housed the Ark in Jerusalem (II Sam. 6:17) in the years before Solomon built the Temple and gave the Ark a place of "rest for ever" (Ps. 132:14). The map shows the circuitous route that took the Ark from Shiloh through its capture by the Philistines, its rescue, and its subsequent placement at Kirjath-jearim (as described in I Sam. 4–6).

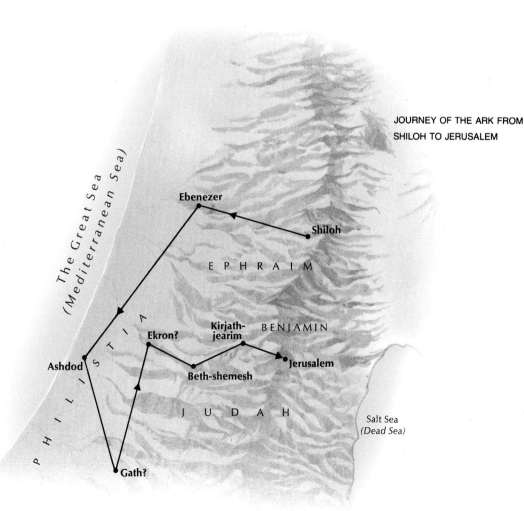

JOURNEY OF THE ARK FROM
SHILOH TO JERUSALEM

... and the pails and the shovels and the bowls; even all these utensils which Hiram made for King Solomon in the house of the Lord were of polished bronze.

1 Kings 7:45

THE MINES OF SOLOMON

Solomon's Temple was furnished with many articles made of bronze, or "brass," as the Hebrew word was rendered at the time of the King James translation. The metal came from Solomon's mines in the region of the Gulf of Aqabah. Unmistakable traces of copper mining and smelting in biblical times—such as slag, crucibles, and the remains of miners' dwellings—have been found in this area. The "Mines of Solomon" are shown here.

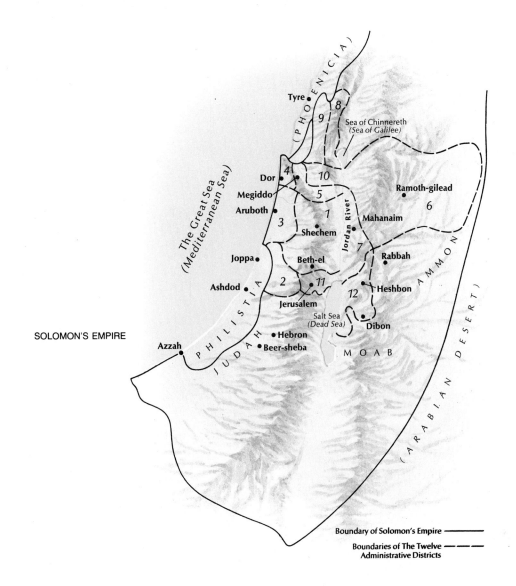

SOLOMON'S EMPIRE

Now Solomon ruled over all the kingdoms from the River to the land of the Philistines and to the border of Egypt; they brought tribute and served Solomon all the days of his life.

1 KINGS 4:21

As ruler "over all kingdoms from the river [the Euphrates] to the land of the Philistines," Solomon inherited from King David more territory than any Israelite king would ever hold again. Within this empire, Solomon controlled the main roads leading from Egypt to Mesopotamia and Anatolia—for all trade between the lush lands of the Nile and the Fertile Crescent passed through his kingdom, and Solomon became the "merchant prince" of his time.
Preserved in the fourth chapter of the First Book of Kings is one of the most important of the royal documents in the Bible: a list of the twelve administrative districts of Solomon's kingdom. The numbers on the map correspond to the districts and their administrators as described in the twelve verses of 1 KINGS 4:8–19. The administration of Judah and of those areas conquered by David is not mentioned.

The king also passed over the brook Kidron, and all the people passed over toward the way of the wilderness.

II SAMUEL 15:23

THE KIDRON VALLEY

The Kidron Valley passes between the Temple mount and the Mount of Olives (1 KINGS 2:37). Starting to the northwest of the Temple mount, it runs into the Dead Sea south of Ain el-Feskhah and Khirbet Qumran. From its bed rises the spring of Gihon (Shiloah), the original source of Jerusalem's water supply. Concealed at the bottom of one of the precipitous gorges of the Judean desert, the Kidron, in its lower course, provided numerous hiding places, and was refuge for fugitives. When David abandoned Jerusalem to Absalom, he and his loyal supporters crossed the Kidron and made their escape into the Judean desert. In the days of the First Temple, the Kidron Valley served as a burial-ground for the inhabitants of Jerusalem (II KIN. 23:6), who shrank from interring their dead in the city. In the time of the Second Temple, this cemetery stretched for over three miles along the Kidron Valley, from the so-called "Tombs of the Judges" at its northern end to south of the Mount of Olives. The most famous of the tombs were "Absalom's Tomb," the Tomb of the priests of the Hezir family (1 CHRON. 24:15), and the Mausoleum of the Adiabene royal family (the "Tombs of the Kings"). The view shows the lower part of the Kidron. From this point the valley runs in front of the southern spur of the Mount of Olives, which can be seen in the background.

38

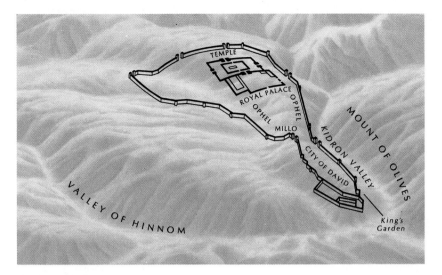

JERUSALEM IN THE TIME OF SOLOMON

Under the rigorous leadership of Solomon, several major cities of Israel were fortified and enlarged—the construction partly financed by taxes ("levy"). Jerusalem, the religious and political center, was the site of his palace and the Temple. These magnificent structures were built adjacent to the City of David, which was on the ridge, scholars generally agree, where the Jebusite city had stood before it was captured by David and his forces (II Sam. 5:6–9). The valley between the city and the Temple mount —the area's highest point—was filled in with earth and named Millo (from the Hebrew verb meaning "to fill"). The city itself was enlarged during Solomon's reign and its wall was relocated, though the exact extent of this expansion is not known; the location of the wall indicated on the map above is approximate, and accords with the views of many scholars. Among the cities Solomon fortified were Hazor, Megiddo, and Gezer. Excavations at these sites have uncovered extensive remains of Solomon's structures. It is likely that they were built following a master plan, for their gates and walls are identical in design.

Now this is the account of the forced labor which King Solomon levied to build the house of the Lord, his own house, the Millo, the wall of Jerusalem, Hazor, Megiddo, and Gezer.

1 KINGS 9:15

At Ezion-geber (Tell el-Kheleifeh), on the gulf of Elath, an ancient settlement has been unearthed. The archaeological finds from the site show that it was once an important industrial center, with a highly efficient metallurgical furnace for the smelting of copper. It is most likely that this industrial center was established by Solomon, the ruler who did so much to develop the crafts, industry, and foreign trade of Israel. It is conjectured that the ore from the mines of the Arabah, after being smelted and refined at Ezion-Geber, constituted the principal commodity exported thence by ship. Some scholars are of the opinion that the expression "ships of Tarshish" (1 Kin. 10:22) refers to large vessels designed for the transport of metals across the sea.

Solomon made use of Tyrian shipbuilders and also of Tyrian sailors who, together with the king's servants, voyaged to countries rich in gold, spices, and precious stones. The ships of Solomon were built on the pattern of Phoenician vessels. A reconstruction of such a vessel, based on reliefs from the 8th century B.C., is reproduced here. The Phoenician ship was larger than its Egyptian counterpart. It was flat-bottomed and had an oblong sail made of sturdy material.

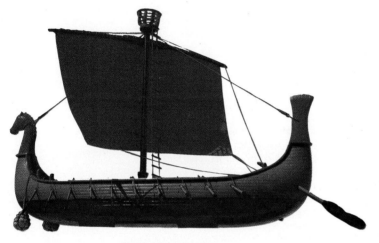

SHIPS OF SOLOMON

For the king had at sea the ships of Tarshish with the ships of Hiram; once every three years the ships of Tarshish came bringing gold and silver, ivory and apes and peacocks.

1 KINGS 10:22

King Solomon also built a fleet of ships in Ezion-geber, which is near Eloth on the shore of the Red Sea, in the land of Edom.

And Hiram sent his servants with the fleet, sailors who knew the sea, along with the servants of Solomon.

1 KINGS 9:26–27

ROUTES OF SOLOMON'S NAVY

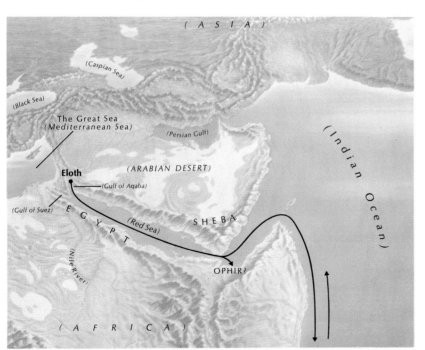

King Hiram of Tyre, in the small state of Phoenicia, entered into a mutually advantageous pact with the increasingly formidable nation of Israel. In addition to timber for the Temple, he sent shipbuilders and sailors to Solomon. The men of Tyre, together with King Solomon's men, sailed to countries rich in gold, spices, and precious stones. And the Tyrians helped build the ships of Solomon on the pattern of Phoenician vessels. In return, Solomon gave to Tyre an annual amount of olive oil and wheat (1 KIN. 5:11), and the Tyrians may also have shared in the profits of Solomon's merchant navy.

HILLS OF SAMARIA

And he bought the hill Samaria from Shemer for two talents of silver; and he built on the hill, and named the city which he built Samaria, after the name of Shemer, the owner of the hill.

1 KINGS 16:24

THE DIVIDED KINGDOM:
ISRAEL AND JUDAH

So Israel has been in rebellion against the house of David to this day.

. . . None but the tribe of Judah followed the house of David.

1 Kings 12:19–20

The immediate cause of the revolt of the ten northern tribes of Israel after King Solomon's death (about 930 B.C.) was the heavy burden of taxes and forced labor he had imposed on the people. Solomon's system of taxation favored his own tribe of Judah and this intensified the antagonism that had existed for many years between the tribes of the north and Judah. But there had also been antagonism between the "House of Joseph" and Judah for many years. While Solomon was still on the throne, Jeroboam, a member of the tribe of Joseph, vainly attempted to foment revolt and had to flee into exile. But after Solomon died, Jeroboam returned to head the kingdom of Israel of the north, as opposed to the kingdom of Judah of the south, which remained loyal to Rehoboam, son of Solomon. Of the three countries David had conquered east of the Jordan, Ammon and Moab became part of Israel; Edom remained part of Judah.

43

TEMPLE OF AMON AT KARNAK

The description given in the Bible of the campaign of Pharaoh Shishak (in Egyptian: Sheshonk) against Rehoboam bears the marks of having been taken from a chronicle of names and dates. The date mentioned here is actually the first in the Bible that can be definitely connected with Egyptian records. An inscription of Shishak, from the southern wall of the temple of Amon at Karnak (see the reproduction), records the Pharaoh's conquests in Palestine (c. 926 B.C.). In the center of the relief stands Amon holding a rope to which captives are bound in rows. Each one of the captives is the ruler of a conquered city, the name of which is engraved on his body within an oval ring. At the right, other captives are seen on their knees, with their hands raised in submission. Although the inscription says nothing at all about the actual course of the war in Palestine, it is possible to reconstruct the Egyptian monarch's line of advance from the detailed list of captured places (about 180 in all). Shishak's forces overran the Negev of Judah and the Kingdom of Israel, taking and sacking many settlements as they went. Jerusalem is not mentioned in the list: it was evidently saved from conquest by the heavy tribute that Rehoboam paid to the Pharaoh. The Bible specifically mentions the deliverance of Jerusalem, attributing it to the submission of the king and his ministers to God's will, as expressed in the words that the Lord put into the mouth of Shemaiah, his prophet: "They have humbled themselves so I will not destroy them, but I will grant them some measure of deliverance, and My wrath shall not be poured out on Jerusalem by means of Shishak" (II CHRON. 12:7).

And there was war between Rehoboam and Jeroboam continually.

1 KINGS 14:30

44

INVASION OF ISRAEL AND JUDAH
BY PHARAOH SHISHAK

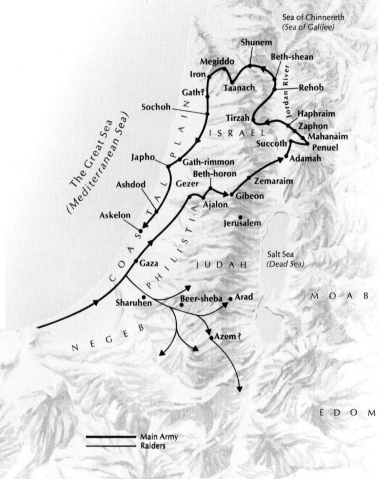

Now it came about in the fifth year of King Rehoboam, that Shishak the king of Egypt came up against Jerusalem.

1 Kings 14:25

Jeroboam, king of the rebellious tribes of Israel in the north, and Rehoboam, king of the southern tribes in Judah, waged wars "all their days" (1 Kin. 14:30). But both these kings had to contend with the powerful Pharaoh Shishak, whose forces about 926 b.c. conquered many cities in the Negev, the coastal plain, the Valley of Succoth (an important strategic base in the time of David and Solomon), the Valley of Jezreel, and the Plain of Sharon. The principal targets of Shishak's invasion are shown on the map.

THE WAY OF THE WILDERNESS OF EDOM

Joram, king of Israel, and Jehoshaphat, king of Judah, accompanied by the king of Edom, who was a vassal of Judah, went to war with Mesha, king of Moab, who had thrown off his allegiance to Israel. As the Jordan fords were blocked by the enemy, the allies advanced upon Moab from the Judean desert, by way of the Arabah, south of the Dead Sea.

On the road to Edom, "the way of the wilderness of Edom" (II KIN. 3:8), the allied armies suffered from a severe shortage of water. They were saved as if by a miracle: in consequence of a sudden flooding the valleys were filled with water, as Elisha had prophesied (II KIN. 3:17). The line followed by "the way of Edom" (see map) can be reconstructed from the remains of fortresses still standing along its course. These include the large fortress of Uzzah in the central hills and a strong watchtower east of it, at the point where the road debouches on to the shore of the Dead Sea. The road descends along Wadi el-Qeini (Valley of the Kenites?), the upper part of which is shown in the photograph, dominated by Uzzah (seen as a line on the horizon in the far background).

For thus says the Lord, 'You shall not see wind nor shall you see rain; yet that valley shall be filled with water, so that you shall drink, both you and your cattle and your beasts.'

2 KINGS 3:17

46

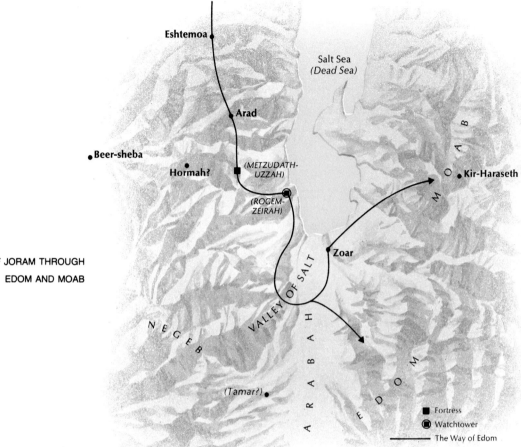

Eshtemoa

Salt Sea
(Dead Sea)

Arad

M
O
A
B

Beer-sheba

Hormah?

(METZUDATH-UZZAH)

Kir-Haraseth

(ROGEM-ZEIRAH)

Zoar

MARCH OF JORAM THROUGH
EDOM AND MOAB

N E G E B

VALLEY OF SALT

A R A B A H

E D O M

(Tamar?)

■ Fortress
◉ Watchtower
━━ The Way of Edom

And he said, "Which way shall we go up?" And he answered, "The way of the wilderness of Edom."

2 Kings 3:8

When King Mesha of Moab withdrew his allegiance from Israel, King Joram of Israel and King Jehoshaphat of Judah, joined by the king of Edom, who was a vassal of Judah, went to war against Moab. As the fords of the Jordan River were blocked by the enemy, the allied forces advanced upon Moab from the Judean desert, by way of the Arabah (Jordan Valley) south of the Dead Sea. On the road to Edom, these armies suffered from a severe shortage of water. They were saved by sudden flooding of the valleys, as Elisha had prophesied (II Kin. 3:16–17). The route of "the way through the wilderness of Edom" (see map) can be reconstructed from the remains of fortresses still standing. These include the large fortress of Uzzah and a watchtower several miles east of it, where the ancient road comes down from the hills to the shore of the Dead Sea.

And Hoshea the son of Elah made a conspiracy against Pekah the son of Remaliah, and struck him and put him to death and became king in his place, in the twentieth year of Jotham the son of Uzziah.   2 KINGS 15:30

About the year 734 B.C., Rezin, king of Aram-Damascus, and Pekah, the son of Remaliah, king of Israel, rose in revolt against Tiglath-pileser III. The Assyrian monarch suppressed the revolt in a series of campaigns in 733–732 B.C. in the course of which he conquered Aram-Damascus and annexed substantial parts of the kingdom of Israel. He took the cities of Galilee, deported most of their inhabitants to Assyria, imposed a heavy tribute upon the remainder, and penetrated deep into Gilead (cf. I CHRON. 5:25–26). The arrows on the map (p. 49) indicate the direction of his various campaigns as reconstructed from Biblical and Assyrian sources. Like the Bible (II KIN. 15:30), Tiglath-pileser relates in his annals that the people of Israel deposed their king Pekah, and adds that he appointed Hoshea to rule over them, with his sovereignty virtually limited to the mountains of Ephraim.

The extent of the devastation of Galilee at that time has been vividly illustrated by the thick layer of ash and charred embers found in the citadel and other buildings at Hazor. The various vessels found still in their places on the floor indicate that the disaster came suddenly. The photograph is a view of the Valley of Beth-Netophah, the site of the ancient cities of Kanah, Arumah, Jotbah, and Hannathon, which are mentioned in a fragment of Tiglath-pileser's annals relating his conquests in Galilee.

THE VALLEY OF BETH-NETOPHAH

Rezin, king of Aram-Damascus, and Pekah, son of King Remaliah of Israel, rose in revolt about 734 B.C. against Tiglath-pileser III of Assyria. In a series of campaigns, the Assyrian monarch defeated the rebels, conquering Aram-Damascus and annexing substantial portions of Israel. The cities of Galilee fell to his army, and he deported most of their inhabitants to Assyria (I CHR. 5:26), forcing those who remained to pay him heavy tribute. Tiglath-pileser's army also penetrated deep into Gilead. The paths of the two armies are reconstructed from biblical and Assyrian sources. As does the Bible (II KIN. 15:30), the official records of Tiglath-pileser III, discovered by archaeologists, report that the people of Israel deposed King Pekah.

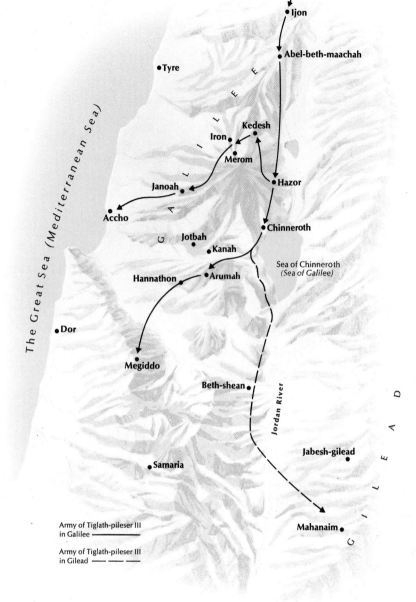

Army of Tiglath-pileser III
in Galilee ——————

Army of Tiglath-pileser III
in Gilead — — — —

CAMPAIGN OF TIGLATH-PILESER III AGAINST SYRIA AND ISRAEL

In the days of Pekah king of Israel, Tiglath-pileser king of Assyria came and captured Ijon and Abelbethmaacah and Janoah and Kedesh and Hazor and Gilead and Galilee, all the land of Naphtali; and he carried them captive to Assyria.   2 KINGS 15:29

THE HABOR RIVER

. . . the king of Assyria captured Samaria and carried Israel away into exile to Assyria, and settled them in Halah and Habor, on the river of Gozan, and in the cities of the Medes.

2 KINGS 17:6

Mentioned among the regions to which the Assyrian king deported the exiles of Samaria is the river Habor, called here also "the river of Gozan" after the principal city on its upper reaches. The Habor flows through a wide plain in northwestern Mesopotamia which is thickly dotted with remains of ancient settlements and crisscrossed with roads (see the view above). Gozan (Tell Halaf) was one of the important Aramaean kingdoms at the beginning of the first millennium B.C. At the end of the 9th century B.C. the city was captured by the Assyrians (cf. II KIN. 19:12), and subsequently became the capital of the Assyrian province of Gozan. It was to this city that many of the exiles from Samaria were deported. Fragments of information about the Israelite deportees have come to light in excavations carried out in various parts of Mesopotamia, especially at Tell Halaf. One of the documents from this city, dating to the 7th century B.C., mentions people bearing names indicative of their Israelite origin: Hoshea, Ishmael, and the woman Dayana (Dinah). A potsherd from the end of the 8th century, or beginning of the 7th century, B.C., discovered at Calah, bears the names, in Aramaic script, of people who must be either Hebrew or Phoenician, e.g.: Hananel, Menahem, Shubael, and Elinur. These were probably deportees from Phoenicia or Israel.

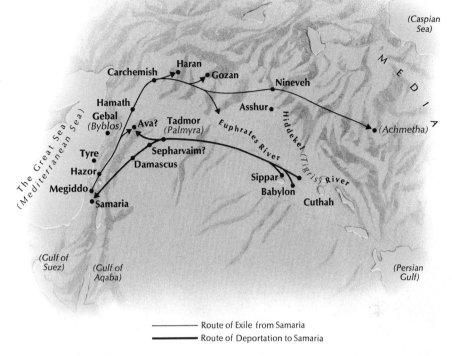

——————— Route of Exile from Samaria
━━━━━━ Route of Deportation to Samaria

TRANSPORT OF CAPTIVE PEOPLES TO AND
FROM SAMARIA BY THE ASSYRIANS

*The Assyrian kings settled the
depopulated regions about Samaria with
foreigners from the southern and
western parts of their empire, after the
Israelites were driven off into exile. The
Bible specifies the places from which
these foreign settlers were deported:
from Babylon and nearby Cuthah and
from the neighboring cities of Ava and
Sepharvaim in Syria (see the heavier
line on the map). Some scholars hold
that Sepharvaim is merely another
name for Sippar in southern
Mesopotamia. In the course of time all
these different nations blended into a
single ethnic and religious entity that
apparently emerged as the Samaritan
community.*

*And the king of Assyria
brought men*

*. . . and settled them in the
cities of Samaria in place of
the sons of Israel. So they
possessed Samaria and lived
in its cities.*

2 KINGS 17:24

REMAINS OF HEROD'S PALACE

In the scroll which was found at Ecbatana, Darius I not only categorically ordered that "the house be rebuilt, the place where sacrifices are offered and burnt—offerings are brought" (EZRA 6:3), but even went so far as to specify the measurements of the new Temple, the vessels that were to be restored to Jerusalem, and the source from which the work was to be financed: "let the cost be paid from the royal treasury". The scroll also lays down the method to be followed in the construction of the Temple—one course of wood to every three courses of heavy stone. This

is probably a reference to the beams (usually of cedar of Lebanon) which were inserted at intervals horizontally into the stone walls, to reinforce the whole structure and give it greater stability. Excavation has shown that this method of building was practiced at Ugarit and in Crete— both of them close to well-wooded areas—as early as the middle of the second millennium B.C. It was also known in Palestine: traces of it have been discovered at Beth-Shan in a building from the end of the Late Bronze Age, and at Megiddo in various structures from the time of Solomon. Some scholars hold that there is a

reference to this method of building in the description of Solomon's Temple: "three courses of hewn stone and one course of cedar beams" (I KINGS 6:36). This architectural design evidently continued in vogue at the time of the return from the Babylonian captivity, and throughout the period of the Second Temple. The picture above is a photograph of the remains of Herod's palace-wall, showing that it had once contained courses of timber. The exceptional preservation of these pieces of wood down the centuries is due to the dry climate of the Judean desert.

. . . with three layers of huge stones, and one layer of timbers. And let the cost be paid from the royal treasury.   EZRA 6:4

Now these are the people of the province who came up out of the captivity of the exiles whom Nebuchadnezzar the king of Babylon had carried away to Babylon, and returned to Jerusalem and Judah, each to his city.

EZRA 2:1

King Cyrus of Persia proved to be a benevolent conqueror after defeating the Babylonians in 538 B.C. He refrained from slaughtering or enslaving his foes, and issued a proclamation allowing the exiles from Judah and other countries to return to their homelands. A similar decree of Cyrus, shown at the top of this page, was found at Babylon. In it, Cyrus tells of rebuilding the temples of his vanquished enemies and restoring the people to their dwelling places. After Cyrus' decree the exiled Jews organized their return to Judah. Those who chose to stay in Babylonia aided those who returned with "a freewill offering for the house of God" (EZRA 1:4). The returning exiles made their way back to Judah in successive waves, starting in the time of Zerubbabel and Jeshua (EZRA 2:1–61; NEH. 7:6–63). The Judah to which they returned was greatly reduced in size from its former days of glory. As the map above shows, it extended no more than twenty-five miles from north to south, and about thirty miles from east to west.

EARLY JEWISH RESETTLEMENT OF JUDAH

53

PALACE OF ARTAXERES II

Now that which was prepared for each day was one ox and six choice sheep, also birds were prepared for me; and once in ten days all sorts of wine were furnished in abundance. Yet for all this I did not demand the governor's food allowance, because the servitude was heavy on this people.

NEHEMIAH 5:18

Nehemiah sharply contrasts his own exemplary probity during his twelve years as governor of Judah with the extortionate practices of the other nobles and officials (NEH. 5:10–13), and also of the former governors who "laid heavy burdens on the people" (ibid., verse 15), and declares that, during his whole term of office, "neither I nor my kinsmen have eaten the governor's food allowance" (ibid., verse 14). The governors who preceded him had, as usual with officials appointed by the Persian government, imposed heavy taxes on the people, and their underlings too had lorded it over the populace, feeding themselves at the latter's expense. Nehemiah's subordinates, on the contrary, were devoted public servants; and Nehemiah himself defrayed the cost of entertaining nobles and officials at his table, quite apart from visitors from beyond the borders of Judah (ibid., verse 17). In a manner reminiscent of the description of "Solomon's provision for one day" (I KIN. 4:22–23), Nehemiah enumerates the quantities of food consumed daily at

So I went up at night by the ravine and inspected the wall. Then I entered the Valley Gate again and returned.

NEHEMIAH 2:15

Nehemiah, cupbearer to the Persian King Artaxerxes, who allowed him to return to Jerusalem as governor of Judah, renewed the walls of the city. The Book of Nehemiah provides us with the probable course of Nehemiah's walls (NEH. 2:14–17; 3; 12:31–39), as well as locations of seven of the city's gates (see map). Thus, we can conjecture as to the route that Nehemiah took when, by night, he surveyed the ruined city (NEH. 2:13). Beginning at the Valley Gate, he traveled to the Dung Gate, climbed the high ground on which the City of David was built, and moved along the sloping terrain of the Kidron Valley as far as the King's Pool (location uncertain). Here the debris became so thick that the animal on which he was riding could go no farther (NEH. 2:14), forcing him to continue on foot. Completing his circuit of the ruined walls, Nehemiah returned to his starting point.

his residence: one bull, six choice sheep, fowls, and wine. It has been calculated that the meat was sufficient to feed eight hundred men, and all at Nehemiah's own expense: "Yet for all this I did not demand the governor's food allowance because the servitude was heavy upon this people" (NEH. 5:18). The kinds of food mentioned in the verse above were also served at the table of the Persian emperors. Reproduced above is a relief from the palace of Artaxerxes II (404–358 B.C.) at Persepolis in which Median and Persian court-attendants are seen bringing a sheep and wine to the king's table. The last of the group is carrying a wineskin.

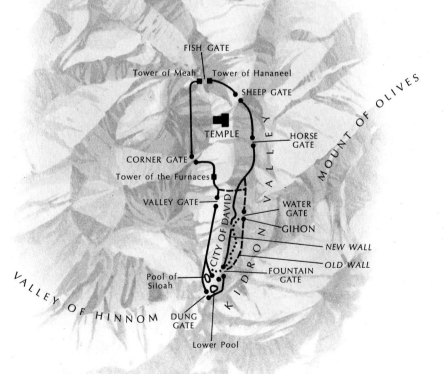

JERUSALEM IN THE TIME OF NEHEMIAH

LACHISH

Among the cities of the coastal plain resettled in Nehemiah's day were Lachish and its fields, and Azekah and its villages. Lachish occupied a strategic position at the approaches to the Hebron hills, southwest of Beth Govrin, and controlled the main highways running from the hill country of Judah down to the Mediterranean coast and the south. In the latter part of the Canaanite period, Lachish was a royal city and an important fortress. Later, in the time of the kingdom of Judah, it repeatedly suffered the ordeal of attack, siege, and destruction, first in the reign of the Assyrian king, Sennacherib, and then in the days of the Babylonian monarch, Nebuchadnezzar. It was finally razed to the ground when the first Temple was destroyed and remained a heap of ruins for about a hundred and fifty years, until it was resettled, together with the other cities of the coastal plain and the Negev. in Nehemiah's day. Preserved on the site are the remains of a public building of this period, which may have been the residence of the Persian governor. The temple of the sun excavated at Lachish—complete with its square court, small cells, steps, and corridors—apparently also belongs to the Persian period. Apart from these two structures, only a few mean houses were uncovered at Lachish dating to the time of the Persian empire.

Lachish and its fields, Azekah and its towns.

NEHEMIAH 11:30

56

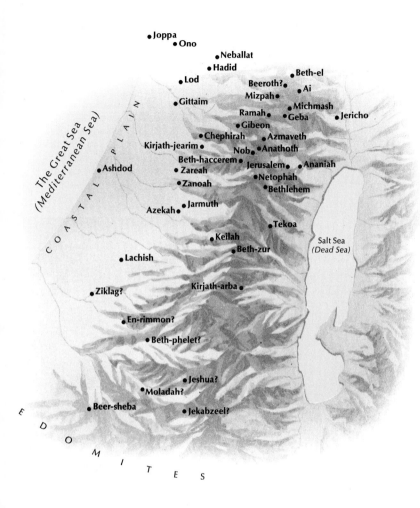

Joppa
Ono
Neballat
Hadid
Beth-el
Lod
Beeroth?
Ai
Mizpah
Gittaim
Michmash
Ramah
Geba
Jericho
Gibeon
Chephirah
Azmaveth
Kirjath-jearim
Nob
Anathoth
Beth-haccerem
Jerusalem
Ananiah
Ashdod
Zareah
Netophah
Zanoah
Bethlehem
Azekah
Jarmuth
Tekoa
Keilah
Salt Sea
(Dead Sea)
Beth-zur
Lachish
Kirjath-arba
Ziklag?
En-rimmon?
Beth-phelet?
Jeshua?
Moladah?
Beer-sheba
Jekabzeel?

The Great Sea
(Mediterranean Sea)

COASTAL PLAIN

EDOMITES

JEWISH OCCUPIED CITIES AFTER THE RETURN

Now these are the heads of the provinces who lived in Jerusalem, but in the cities of Judah each lived on his own property in their cities—

NEHEMIAH 11:3

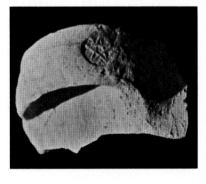

From the first return of the Jewish exiles to Jerusalem until Nehemiah's day—about a century—the population of Judah steadily increased and more places in the hill country and on the coastal plain were resettled, as shown in the map. This Jewish resettlement eventually burst the narrow limits of the Persian province to which the first exiles had returned and overflowed into other parts of Palestine (NEH. 11:25–36). Jerusalem, a desolate ruin at the time of the return, now became a great city once again. In the generation following Nehemiah, Jerusalem enjoyed considerable economic prosperity and rose to be an administrative and religious center. Above is a seal impression found in the excavations at Ramat Rahel, near Jerusalem, on which can be seen a five-pointed star with five letters, Y-R-Sh-L-M, between the points, together making up the word "Yerushalem" (Jerusalem). This inscription, and similar ones found stamped on the handles of clay vessels, bear witness to Jerusalem's special status in the 4th century B.C.

A decree marked with the seal of Ahasuerus' authority was issued from Susa revoking the order for the extermination of the Jews. Though Esther and Mordecai wrote the decree, the imprint of the king's ring gave it the force of absolute law (ESTH. 8:8–10). Susa was the principal residence of Darius and Xerxes, though during the summer the royal court moved to the more pleasing climate of Persepolis. From the ruins of Susa (photograph at the bottom of the page) archaeologists have unearthed a number of beautifully worked stone capitals, topped by two bulls (below), which supported the wood beams of the palace roof. These capitals closely resemble those atop pillars standing on the site of Xerxes' audience hall at Persepolis.

So the king commanded that it should be done so; and an edict was issued in Susa, and Haman's ten sons were hanged.

ESTHER 9:14

SUSA

58

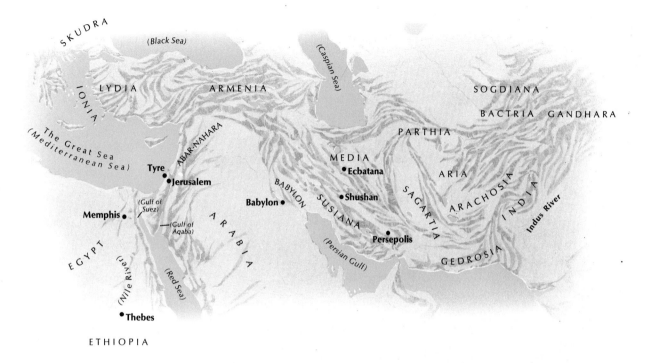

THE PERSIAN EMPIRE UNDER DARIUS

*N*ow *it took place in the days of Ahasuerus, the Ahasuerus who reigned from India to Ethiopia over 127 provinces*

. . . in the third year of his reign, he gave a banquet for all his princes and attendants, the army officers of Persia and Media, the nobles, and the princes of his provinces being in his presence. ESTHER 1:1–3

The Book of Esther tells the dramatic story of the efforts of Mordecai and his cousin Esther to save their fellow Jews from annihilation at the hands of Ahasuerus, ruler of the far-flung Persian Empire. From inscriptions on palace walls of his capital at Persepolis most scholars conclude that the biblical Ahasuerus was the famous Xerxes (486–465 B.C.), renowned for his wars against the Greeks. According to the verses at the left, the Persian Empire extended from "India to Ethiopia." Modern historians agree, explaining that "India" refers only to the area surrounding the Indus River and "Ethiopia" is really the Nubia of ancient times. Persian sources indicate that Darius the Great, father of Xerxes, ruled some twenty satrapies (shown on the map). These were subdivided into provinces, one of which was Judah at the time of Jerusalem's reconstruction. The precise boundaries of the 127 provinces of Ahasuerus (ESTH. 1:1) are for the most part unknown. Sometime during his reign, Ahasuerus gave a great banquet for the princes and governors of his realm (ESTH. 1:3), perhaps to celebrate a dual event—his birthday and the Persian New Year.

BABYLONIAN CHRONICLE

Under Nebuchadnezzar, who ascended the throne in 604 B.C., the Babylonians finally wrested the control of Syria and Palestine from the Egyptians. Jehoiachin had reigned for only three months when Nebuchadnezzar captured Jerusalem and despoiled the treasuries of the Temple and of the royal palace. Jehoiachin was taken into captivity together with the members of his court, the minister, the craftsmen, the smiths, and all the military commanders. A Babylonian chronicle from the time of Nebuchadnezzar confirms the biblical account of the surrender of Jerusalem in Jehoiachin's reign and the enthroning of Zedekiah by the Babylonian monarch (II KIN. 24:8–17; II CHRON. 36:9–10): "And he (i.e., Nebuchadnezzar) encamped against the city of Judah (i.e., Jerusalem), and in the month of Adar, on the second day, he captured the city and took the king prisoner. A king of his own choice he set up in its midst; its heavy tribute he received and carried it off to Babylon." This inscription provides us with the exact date when Jerusalem fell, the second of Adar (March 16), at the end of the seventh year of Nebuchadnezzar's reign (597 B.C.; JER. 52:28). However, the deportation of the Judeans to Babylon took place some time later, in Nebuchadnezzar's eighth year (II KIN. 24:12).

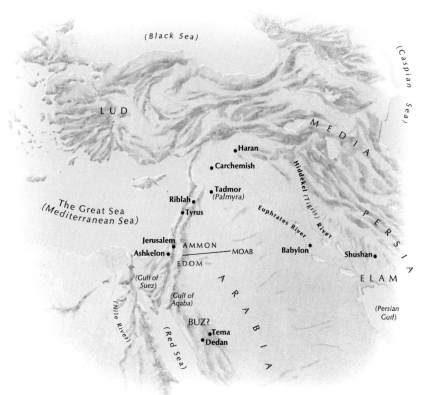

THE BABYLONIAN EMPIRE
UNDER NEBUCHADNEZZAR

This map shows the Babylonian Empire at the height of its power. In Jeremiah's time, the Assyrian Empire declined as the Babylonians reached their greatest strength. To the prophet, these events were a sign of divine providence, and Nebuchadnezzar (Nebuchadrezzar) was an instrument of the Lord's purpose. In a prophecy uttered in "the first year of Nebuchadnezzar" (JER. 25:1)—605 or 604 B.C.—Jeremiah told of the conquests of the Babylonian king. Presumably Jeremiah spoke when the Babylonians were attacking the land west of the Euphrates. A Babylonian chronicle gives a consecutive list of places that fell to Nebuchadnezzar— among them certain of the nations that Jeremiah commanded to drink "this cup of the wine of wrath" (JER. 25:15–26): Judah and Philistia, the Arabian tribes, and Elam.

I will send and take all the families of the north,' declares the Lord, 'and I will send to Nebuchadnezzar king of Babylon, My servant, and will bring them against this land, and against its inhabitants, and against all these nations round about; and I will utterly destroy them, and make them a horror, and a hissing, and an everlasting desolation.

JEREMIAH 25:9

"And I shall set fire to the temples of the gods of Egypt

JEREMIAH 43:12

Jeremiah prophesied that Nebuchadnezzar would overrun Egypt, dealing out slaughter and destruction and desecrating the temples of the Egyptian gods (JER. 43:11–13). Ezekiel, too, similarly foretold the defeat of Egypt by the Babylonian monarch. Both these prophecies came true, at least in part, as is testified by a Babylonian inscription which describes an invasion of Egypt by Nebuchadnezzar in 568–567 B.C. and his war against the Pharaoh Amasis.

Josephus also records a campaign of Nebuchadnezzar against Egypt (Antiquities x.9.7). But the actual conquest of Egypt was not accomplished until a later date, by the Persian king Cambyses. A good idea of the appearance and size of the shrines whose destruction by fire was prophesied by Jeremiah may be obtained from the hall of pillars in the temple of Amon at Karnak, which was built during the reigns of Seti I and Ramses II (13th century B.C.). The

center of the hall is occupied by two parallel rows of pillars, six to a row, each pillar being sixty-nine feet high. On either side of this central nave there are another sixty-one columns, each about forty-two feet high, making one hundred and twenty-two in all. All these pillars are ornamented and covered with hieroglyphic inscriptions (see the photograph). These gigantic monuments survived even the devastation of the cities of ancient Egypt.

TEMPLE OF AMON

The Great Sea *(Mediterranean Sea)*

●**Migdol?**

●**Tahapanes**

●**Pi-beseth**

Lower Egypt

●**Beth-shemesh**

(SINAI

PENINSULA)

Noph ●

E
G
Y
P
T

(Gulf of Suez)

(Gulf of Aqaba)

(Red Sea)

(Nile River)

●**Abydos**

●**No**

Upper Egypt

●*(Aswan)*

●*(Elephantine)*

CITIES OF JEWISH SETTLEMENT IN EGYPT

At the time of the destruction of Solomon's Temple by the Babylonians (586 B.C.), Jews were settled in numerous Egyptian cities (see map). Ancient manuscripts and other evidence found at these sites and elsewhere confirm that immigrants from Judah lived in Egypt as early as the 6th century B.C. Writings in Aramaic—the language of the Judeans—form a key part of this evidence. Shown above is an Aramaic papyrus manuscript, telling of the rituals observed in the shrine of the Judean community at Elephantine in the 5th century B.C.

The word that came to Jeremiah for all the Jews living in the land of Egypt, those who were living in Migdol, Tahpanhes, Memphis, and the land of Pathros

JEREMIAH 44:1

MOAB

In the oracle concerning Moab the devastation of the country and the headlong, panic-stricken flight of its inhabitants is depicted in vivid poetic images (JER. 48:2–10, 15–25). No part of the land, neither valley nor plain, will be spared: "And a destroyer will come to every city, so that no city will escape; the valley also will be ruined, and the plateau will be destroyed" (JER. 48:8). Hordes of refugees will stream southward toward the Arnon, fleeing from the ravages of the invader. But there will be no escape even for those who dwell in seeming security beside its banks. The river Arnon, which, together with its tributary the Heidan, encircles the territory of Dibon, flows through a steep, twisting gorge in the mountains of Moab. As the natural defense of the heart of the country it was of great strategic importance. In times of political decline, the kingdom of Moab shrank to the area on the southern side of the river, which thus became its natural border on the north. But, in its more vigorous and prosperous periods, the kingdom again expanded northward beyond the river. The photograph shows the powerful grandeur imprinted upon the desert landscape of Transjordan by the deep canyons of the Arnon.

Moab has been put to shame, for it has been shattered. JEREMIAH 48:20

Concerning Moab.

Thus says the Lord of hosts, the God of Israel, "Woe to Nebo, for it has been destroyed; Kiriathaim has been put to shame, it has been captured.

JEREMIAH 48:1

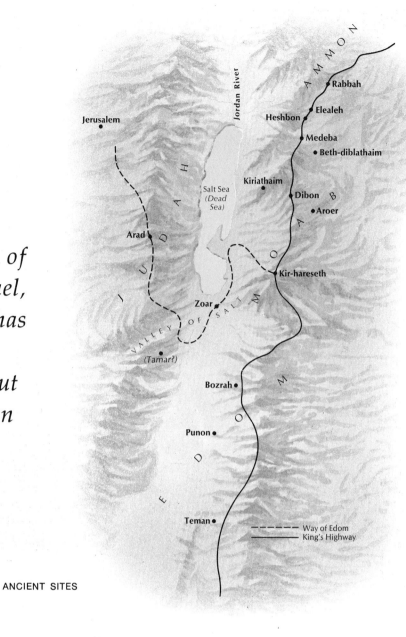

ANCIENT SITES

Jeremiah's prophecies against the enemies of Israel east of the Jordan—Moab, Ammon, and Edom—contain ancient ballads about various disasters suffered by these kingdoms during their long histories (JER. 48 and 49:1–22). There are similar pronouncements concerning Moab in the Book of Isaiah (compare JER. 48:1–8, 29–36 with IS. 15:1–7) and in Obadiah's vision about Edom (compare JER. 49:7–11, 14–17 with the Book of Obadiah). All these passages apparently have a common origin in the works of ancient bards and prophets (NUM. 21:27–30). Many places mentioned in these Old Testament passages as cities in the lands directly across the Jordan can, as a result of archaeological surveys, be identified today. They are plotted on the map above.

Damascus

Mount Hermon

PHOENICIA

Caesarea Philippi

Sidon

Zarephath

Tyre

Bethsaida

Chorazin

Capernaum

Ptolemais

GALILEE

(Sea of Galilee)

(PLAIN OF GENNESARET)

Tiberias

Magdala

MOUNTAINS OF GALILEE

Cana

Nazareth

Mount Tabor

Nain

Mount Carmel

Gadara?

Gerasa

D E C A P O L I S

Jordan River

(PEREA)

Mount Gilboa

Mount Ebal

Sychar

Shechem

Samaria

Mount Gerizim

SAMARIA

Jericho

Ephraim

Beth-el

Beth.

Mount of O

Jerusalem

Bethlehem

Arimathea

Lydda

Emmaus

Joppa

Azotus

Ashke

Caesarea

(Mediterranean Sea)

THE MINISTRY OF JESUS

A grove of trees (left) on the northwestern shore of the Sea of Galilee, just below the mouth of the Jordan, today marks the site of Capernaum—a bustling fishing village in the time of Jesus. He chose Capernaum as his home during his Galilean ministry. Although Jesus was apparently disappointed by Capernaum's response to his teachings (MT. 11:23–24), the village and its surrounding countryside had yielded five of his twelve apostles—Matthew, the brothers Simon (Peter) and Andrew, and the brothers James and John—and it is referred to as "his own city" (MT. 9:1). The map shows the Holy Land in the time of Jesus and locates many of the villages, towns, and cities that the Gospels of Matthew, Mark, Luke, and John tell us he visited. Jesus was born in Bethlehem (MT. 2:1; LK. 2:4–7), and soon afterward Joseph and Mary fled

with Jesus to Egypt (not shown) to escape the massacre of the infants ordered by King Herod (MT. 2:13–16). They lived in Egypt for approximately two years before returning to Nazareth, the Galilean city in which Joseph and Mary had lived before going to Bethlehem. There Jesus grew to manhood. At the age of twelve he was taken to Jerusalem, where he amazed the teachers of the Law with his knowledge of Scripture (LK. 2:41–52). John the Baptist, preaching up and down the Jordan Valley, proclaimed Jesus the Messiah and baptized him in the river (MT. 3:13–17; MK. 1:9–11; LK. 3:21–22; JN. 1:29–33). Precisely where Jesus was baptized is not certain; in John 1:28 it is called "Bethany beyond Jordan" and may have been Beth-barah, a town mentioned in the Old Testament (JUDG. 7:24), which stood at the edge of the Judean

. . . and leaving Nazareth, He came and settled in Capernaum.

From that time Jesus began to preach and say, "Repent, for the kingdom of heaven is at hand." MATTHEW 4:13, 17

wilderness. After his baptism Jesus wandered in this barren region for forty days (MT. 4:1–11; MK. 1:12–13; LK. 4:1–13). Emerging from the wilderness, he found his first followers—Andrew, Peter, Philip, and Nathaniel—and started back to Galilee. Stopping at Cana on the way, Jesus performed the first of many miracles by changing water to wine (JN. 2:1–11). At the end of this journey Jesus arrived at Capernaum. From there he went out into the Galilean countryside preaching and performing miracles, followed by multitudes. Here, in the land where he had been raised, Jesus spent much of the rest of his life; many of the most momentous events of his ministry occurred in Galilee. Near Capernaum he named twelve of his followers to become his apostles (MT. 10:1–4; MK. 3:13–19; LK. 6:12–16) and delivered the Sermon on the Mount (MT. 5:1–8; LK.

6:20–49). At Nazareth he was rejected and forced to flee for his life (MT. 13:54–58; MK. 6:1–6; LK. 4:16–30). At nearby Nain he raised a widow's son from the dead (LK. 7:11–17) and at Bethsaida healed a blind man (MK. 8:22–26). Across the Sea of Galilee he restored two Gadarene demoniacs to their senses (MT. 8:28–34; see also MK. 5:1–20 and LK. 8:26–39). The Sea of Galilee itself was the scene of several of Jesus' miracles. While crossing from Capernaum to its eastern shore, he stilled a tempest that threatened to swamp the small boat in which he and his disciples were sitting (MT. 8:23–27; MK. 4:35–41; LK. 8:22–25); and Jesus walked upon the water of this sea (MT. 14:22–23; MK. 6:45–52; JN. 6:15–21). On the northeastern shore of Galilee Jesus performed the miracle of the loaves and fishes, feeding a vast crowd that had come to hear him (MT. 14:13–21; MK. 6:30–44; LK. 9:10–17; JN. 6:1–14). Although Jesus concentrated most of his energies on preaching in Galilee, he and his disciples traveled widely in nearby regions. They went north into Phoenicia, in the region of the coastal cities of Tyre and Sidon, where Jesus healed a Canaanite's daughter (MT. 15:21–28; MK. 7:24–30). In the Decapolis, an area controlled by several cities that had been united by the Roman conqueror Pompey, Jesus performed several miracles, including the feeding of a great multitude (MT. 15:32–38; MK. 8:1–9). Near Caesarea Philippi the Transfiguration took place: Jesus revealed his true nature to his three most trusted

disciples—Peter, James, and John—and foretold his death and Resurrection (MT. 17:1–13; MK. 9:2–13; LK. 9:28–36). Different traditions place the Transfiguration upon Mount Hermon or Mount Tabor. In addition to his journeys to neighboring lands, Jesus traveled from Galilee to Jerusalem for the annual religious observances. He made several such journeys during his adult life, the initial one soon after reaching Galilee from the wilderness to begin his ministry. During this visit he drove the money changers from the Temple (JN. 2:13–18) and on his way back first made known his mission on earth to a Samaritan woman whom he met at a well near Sychar (JN. 4:4–42). After a time in Galilee, Jesus set out for the last trip to Jerusalem, journeying through Judea and Peraea, and preaching all along the way. He stayed in Peraea for a time, making a brief visit to Bethany, where he raised his friend Lazarus from the dead (JN. 11:1–44). From Peraea Jesus moved on toward Jerusalem, stopping at Jericho, where he healed two blind men (MT. 20:29–34; see also MK. 10:46–52 and LK. 18:35–43) and converted Zaccheus, a wealthy publican (LK. 19:1–10). From Jericho Jesus went again to Bethany, where he was anointed by Mary, the sister of Lazarus (MT. 26:6–13; MK. 14:3–9; JN. 12:1–8), and then made his last triumphant entrance into Jerusalem (MT. 21:1–11; MK. 11:1–11; LK. 19:28–40; JN. 12:12–19). (For a map of Jerusalem, the scene of Jesus' agony on the Cross and his final victory, see page 69.)

Upon leaving the Temple, Jesus and his disciples would have passed through one of the gateways in the massive retaining walls that Herod the Great had built around the Temple. Portions of the Herodian walls stand to this day. The view here is along the south wall, from the corner overlooking the Kidron Valley, which Jesus and his disciples would have crossed on their way to the Mount of Olives. The Herodian stones are in the lower, more prominent rows. These giant blocks of hewn stone are from 9 to 15 feet long and 3 to 4 feet high. The largest is 36 feet long; the heaviest weighs nearly 100 tons. Herod began rebuilding the Temple about 20 B.C.

HEROD'S STONES

And as He was going out of the temple, one of His disciples said to Him, "Teacher, behold what wonderful stones and what wonderful buildings!"

MARK 13:1

And when they had come to a place called Golgotha, which means Place of a Skull,

And when they had crucified Him, they divided up His garments among themselves, casting lots;

MATTHEW 27:33, 35

JERUSALEM AT THE TIME OF THE CRUCIFIXION

Condemned by Pilate to be crucified, Jesus was led from the governor's residence to the place of execution at Golgotha. The specific location of this "place of a skull" is not known. Some traditions locate it on the site of the present-day Church of the Holy Sepulcher. In the time of Jesus the Romans made public spectacles of executions to impress upon the people the fate that might await anyone who broke the laws of the empire. Executions were often held near city gates so that passersby could see them as they went in and out of the city. Because there are no suitable flat surfaces near the south, west, and east walls that then surrounded Jerusalem, some scholars believe that Golgotha must have been as shown on the map, somewhere on the fairly flat land near the city's north wall. The possessions of those condemned to death were usually confiscated by the state. But the few things the destitute had were often left to the guards and executioners; what could not be divided was gambled for. The Roman soldiers who cast lots for Jesus' garments probably did so by flipping a coin or by rolling dice—two forms of gambling common to the times. A 6th century B.C. Greek vase (right) illustrates another ancient form of gambling: playing checkers for a stake.

TIBERIAS ON THE SEA OF GALILEE

The Sea of Galilee, or Lake Gennesaret, is undoubtedly the geographical center of Jesus' activity in Galilee. Here another of its names is mentioned: "Sea of Tiberias" after the principal Galilean city situated on its shores. This is the name preserved in Jewish tradition (Yamma shel Tiberya-Tosephta Sukka 3:9) and by the Arabs, who call the lake Bahr Tabariyeh, the Sea of Tiberias.

Tiberias is one of the few cities in the Holy Land which have kept their Roman name; this happened because the city was founded in Roman times and entirely superseded the previously existing village of Rakkath (JOSH. 19:35). Tiberias was founded by Herod Antipas, the tetrarch, in honor of the emperor Tiberius, most probably in A.D. 18. In the time of Jesus' mission it was therefore quite a new city. The Herodian town was situated south of the present-day Old City of Tiberias; part of its area is shown in the photograph. The line of walling in the background is the 18th century southern wall of Tiberias, which was built on the foundation of the northern wall of the Roman city. Constructed on a lavish scale and inhabited by a mixed population of fishermen and artisans, Tiberias soon became one of the largest and most prosperous cities on the lake; and it has retained this position, owing to the decline of its only rival, Taricheae-Migdal. As the other cities bordering the lake (Gadara, Susitha-Hippos) are at some distance from its waters, it rightly took its name from Tiberias.

After these things Jesus went away to the other side of the Sea of Galilee (or Tiberias). JOHN 6:1

And when he learned that He belonged to Herod's jurisdiction, he sent Him to Herod, who himself also was in Jerusalem at that time.

LUKE 23:7

This map depicts the political divisions of the Holy Land during the last years of Jesus' earthly life. When Pilate, the Roman governor of Judea and Samaria, learned that Jesus was a citizen of Nazareth in Galilee, he sent him before the ruler of Galilee, Herod Antipas, who was one of the sons of Herod the Great. With Rome's help Herod the Great had ruled all of the Holy Land except the southern desert areas, which were under Nabatean rule, the coastal cities of Ashkelon and Ptolemais, and most of the Decapolis, a league of cities established by Pompey in 63 B.C. After Herod's death his kingdom was divided among his sons: Archelaus (who received Judea and Samaria), Philip, and Herod Antipas. Archelaus was later deposed, and his territory was controlled by a series of Roman governors, of whom Pontius Pilate was one.

POLITICAL DIVISION OF THE HOLY LAND

IN THE TIME OF JESUS

THIRD CENTURY PAPYRUS

As is shown by the preface to the Book of Acts, this history of the early Christian movement is a sequel to the Gospel of Luke. Both are dedicated to a man named Theophilus, and are written in the same skillful literary style. As its title suggests, here is the very beginning of the story of the Church in action, set down by an eyewitness of at least some of the events and a participant in the transformation of a small Palestinian sect to a world religion, spreading across the Orient until it reached Rome herself. At first the story is concerned with events in Jerusalem: the replacement of Judas to reconstitute the Twelve; Pentecost; the emergence of Peter as the leader of the Christian community in its early days; and the martyrdom of Stephen, the leader of the new "deacons," for his ardent public preaching. Then the scope broadens: Philip is dispatched and converts a eunuch of the queen of Ethiopia on his southward journey home. But it is with the conversion of Saul of Tarsus that the appeal to the Gentiles begins in earnest. Geographic expansion was accompanied by internal problems within the Jerusalem Church, with attendant discussions about the validity of the Jewish Law, as regards both converted Jews and Gentiles who adopted Christianity. Starting with ch. 16, where Luke apparently joins Paul's missionary team, the chronology becomes firmer; many scholars believe that the second half of Acts is in effect based upon Luke's travel diary. More and more the narrative concerns itself with the mission to the Greeks and the Romans, of which Paul was the agent, and with his activities: his arrest at Jerusalem, transfer to Caesarea, his appeal to the emperor as a Roman citizen, and his voyage to the imperial city. There the story ends. The account can be well fitted into the general historical framework of the period; and, despite certain discrepancies with Paul's own account of certain events, as found in his Epistles, can be confirmed to a large extent from exterior sources. The illustration is from a third-century papyrus of the Acts, containing vv. 23:11–16, 24–29; it was found at Oxyrhynchus, Egypt, and is now in the Laurentian Library, Florence.

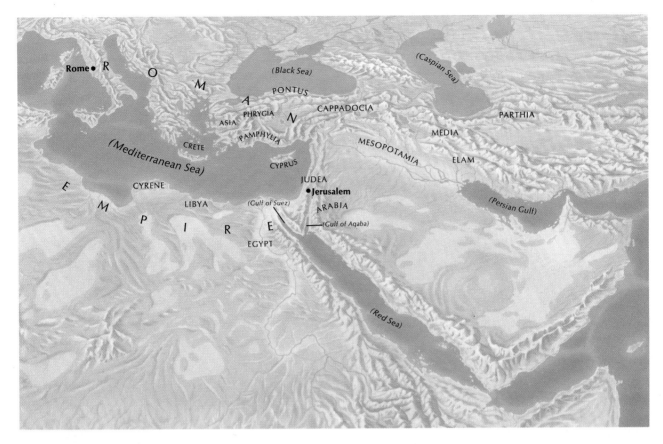

THE DIASPORA

Cretans and Arabs—we hear them in our own tongues speaking of the mighty deeds of God. ACTS 2:11

Luke, a convert to Christianity, writes in Acts 1 of the events that immediately preceded and followed the Ascension of Christ, and of the meaning of the Resurrection. In Acts 2 the ministry of the apostles begins as Jewish pilgrims from many nations assemble in Jerusalem on Pentecost and hear of "the wonderful works of God." The biblical account of the Jewish Diaspora—the lands to which the Jews had emigrated from Palestine by the 1st century A.D.—is given in Acts 2:9–11; these lands are shown on the map above. A great many Jews lived in northeastern Africa in the time of Jesus, especially in Egypt, and also in Libya and Cyrene.

The "Arabians" were probably Jews living in the Nabatean kingdom. The "strangers of Rome" were Jews (mostly descendants of captives brought to Rome) and proselytes (converts to Judaism). The presence of proselytes in Jerusalem is attested to by the inscription in Greek at the left, from a 1st century A.D. burial casket found there. It reads, "Judatos, (son of) the proselyte Laganion." The rest of Acts tells of the founding of the early Church—how a few men from Palestine traveled through that very empire whose officials had caused their Master to be crucified.

73

ANTIOCH

From chapter 11 onward, the Acts are almost exclusively concerned with the activity of Paul, from the moment Barnabas brought him to Antioch to his arrival in Rome. Antioch was founded in 301 by Seleucus I Nicator, the first king of the Seleucid dynasty, and was so called in honor of his father, Antiochus. It remained the capital of the kingdom of Syria till its annexation by the Romans, and continued to be the capital of the Roman province of Syria. The site was most judiciously chosen, in the broad valley of the river Orontes, with mountains protecting the city on the south. Nearby was the famous pleasure-resort of Daphne. In the period with which the Acts deal, Antioch was the third largest city of the Roman Empire and was famous for its luxury and the mordant wit of its population. A Jewish community had existed there since the foundation of the city; in the time of Demetrius II the Jews helped to suppress a local uprising. The large Jewish community in Antioch in Roman times served as the base for the preaching of Barnabas and Paul, who labored there for a long time; it was here that the community for the first time adopted the name "Christians," i.e., followers of Christos, the "Anointed One" or Messiah. In later times Antioch was the seat of a Patriarch, the head of all the churches in the Orient. The present town of Antioch (Antakiye, in the Turkish province of Hatay) is a small place situated within the vast enclosure of the ancient walls. Excavations have so far uncovered only a small part of the city's rich remains.

. . . and when he had found him, he brought him to Antioch

ACTS 11:26

74

So, being sent out by the Holy Spirit, they went down to Seleucia and from there they sailed to Cyprus.

And when they reached Salamis, they began to proclaim the word of God in the synagogues.

ACTS 13:4–5

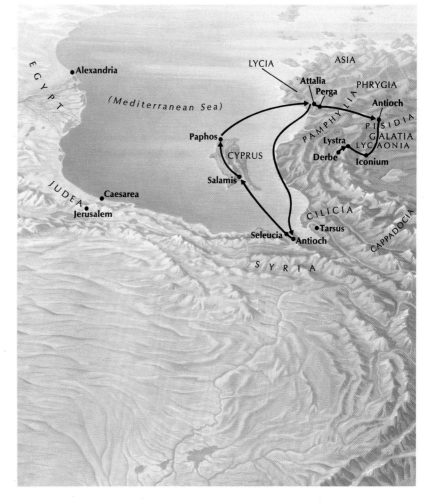

PAUL'S FIRST MISSIONARY JOURNEY

In A.D. 47 Saul and Barnabas—along with John, "whose surname was Mark," a young follower and nephew of Barnabas—set out on a missionary journey to Cyprus. Landing at Salamis, they preached in synagogues across the island. At Paphos, the Roman proconsul, Sergius Paulus, was converted and the sorcerer Elymas, who had tried to stop their preaching, was struck blind (ACTS 13:6–12). From Paphos, the missionaries set sail for the southern coast of Asia Minor, landing on the shore of Pamphylia. At Perga, John Mark disappointed Paul, as Saul now called himself (ACTS 13:9), by deserting his companions and returning to Jerusalem (ACTS 13:13; 15:37–39). Paul and Barnabas went on without him, visiting cities in the regions of Pisidia and Lycaonia of the Roman province of Galatia. In Pisidian Antioch, Paul preached a sermon that is the earliest of his recorded in the Bible (ACTS 13:16–41). At Lystra, Paul was stoned and left for dead by an angry crowd (ACTS 14:19). At Derbe, the two missionaries turned around and, revisiting the fledgling churches of Asia Minor, made their way back to Syrian Antioch in A.D. 49.

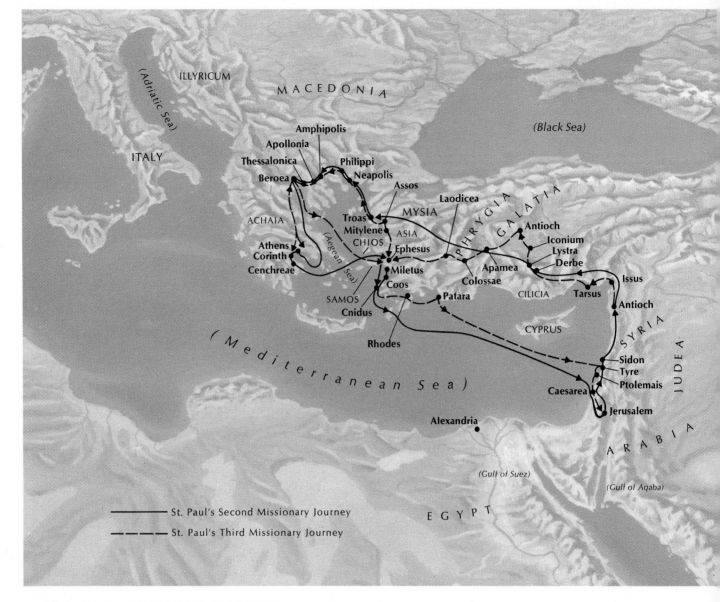

PAUL'S SECOND AND THIRD MISSIONARY JOURNEYS

Paul's second journey began, in A.D. 49, where his first ended, at Antioch in Syria. Accompanied by his assistant Silas (ACTS 15:40), Paul first traveled by land through Syria and Cilicia, visiting and reassuring the churches of Asia Minor, which had been founded on his first journey (see page 75). He asked Timothy to join him (ACTS 16:1–3), and, together with Silas, they walked on through Galatia and Phrygia. Along the way the Holy Spirit forbade them to preach in the province of Asia (ACTS 16:6), causing them to travel north, into Mysia. At Troas, Paul met Luke, the "beloved physician" (COL. 4:14) and author of ACTS, who joined the party. Here Paul had a vision of a Macedonian beckoning him to come and preach in his land (ACTS 16:9). Setting sail from Troas (ACTS

16:11), Paul and his companions crossed the Aegean Sea, landed at Neapolis in Macedonia, and then traveled inland to Philippi (ACTS 16:12). Here the first church in Europe was founded. Here, too, an angry crowd seized Paul and Silas and had them thrown into jail (ACTS 16:19–24). An earthquake—and Paul's Roman citizenship—brought about their release the next morning (ACTS 16:25–40). From Philippi, the missionaries traveled through Amphipolis and Apollonia. Paul stayed for some time at Thessalonica, and many Greeks were converted, but he was again forced to flee from angered Jews (ACTS 17:1–9). At nearby Beroea, Paul was so successful in preaching to Jews as well as Gentiles that the Jewish leaders of Thessalonica forced him to move on

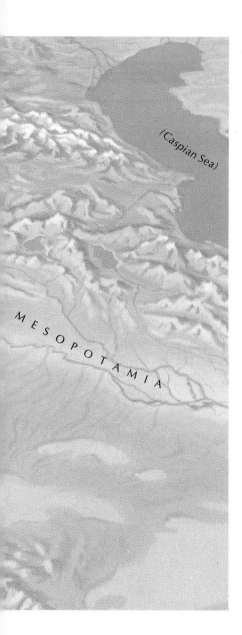

(Caspian Sea)

MESOPOTAMIA

And when he had landed at Caesarea, he went up and greeted the church, and went down to Antioch.

. . . And having spent some time there, he departed and passed successively through the Galatian region and Phrygia, strengthening all the disciples. ACTS 18:22–23

(ACTS 17:10–13). Leaving his companions at Beroea, Paul went to Athens (ACTS 17:14–15). Here he preached with such eloquence that he was invited to speak before a distinguished gathering on the Areopagus that included Epicureans and Stoics (ACTS 17:18–34). At Corinth, the next stop on his long journey, the apostle stayed eighteen months, dwelling with recent converts. His success in Corinth, especially among the poor and uneducated (I COR. 1:26), brought him to the attention of devout Jews who complained to the Roman authorities that he was preaching an unauthorized faith (ACTS 18:12–17). Notwithstanding the proconsul's speedy dismissal of this charge, Paul soon left Corinth. Pausing at Ephesus, the original goal of his

journey, he promised its people that he would return there one day (ACTS 18:19–21), and sailed on to Caesarea. He went to visit the church at Jerusalem and then returned to Antioch (ACTS 18:22) in A.D. 52. Setting out once again from Antioch in A.D. 53, Paul first retraced his steps in Asia Minor, revisiting many of the churches founded on his earlier journeys. Crossing the western mountains, he eventually reached Ephesus (ACTS 19:1), the capital of the province of Asia, fulfilling the promise he had made to return. He lived and worked in Ephesus for more than two years, preaching first to the Jews and then —when no more of them responded—to the Gentiles (ACTS 19:10). Paul was persecuted by unbelievers (ACTS 20:19) and was the cause of a riot that forced him to leave the city. He then made his way to Troas and cities in Macedonia, preaching to their Christian communities. Reaching the southern border of Illyricum (ROM. 15:19), he journeyed south to Corinth, where he spent three months (ACTS 20:2–3). To symbolize the ties of faith that united Christians everywhere, Paul asked that a collection be made from all the churches he had helped establish, to be presented to the poor Christians of Judea at Jerusalem. Setting out from Corinth in the winter of A.D. 57, Paul traveled by land to Philippi (where Luke joined him) and then to Troas (ACTS 20:6), where he met delegates from all the churches and received from them their portions of the collection.

Funds in hand, Paul and his party set out for Jerusalem, stopping first at Miletus, where the leaders of the church at Ephesus came to bid Paul farewell (ACTS 20:13–38). At Tyre (ACTS 21:3–4) and at Caesarea (ACTS 21:10–13), Christian prophets warned Paul not to go to Jerusalem. Their unheeded warnings proved accurate. At first all went well: Paul was warmly greeted by the elders of the church, and his offering was gratefully received. But, as a gesture of goodwill toward those Christians of Judea who, like himself, had been converted from Judaism, Paul went to the Temple to perform Jewish rituals (ACTS 21:26). An angry mob quickly gathered and would have killed Paul if Roman soldiers had not intervened, putting the apostle under arrest until their commander could discover what was behind the disturbance (ACTS 21:27–36). The Romans brought Paul before the Jewish council of elders. His assertion that he was a Pharisee led to a dispute between the Pharisees and the Sadducees that made a verdict impossible (ACTS 23:1–10). When the Romans learned that there was a plot afoot to lynch Paul, they took him under heavy guard to Caesarea (ACTS 23:12–35). Thereafter, for at least four years, Paul was a prisoner of the Romans. Despite his argument that he had never intended to profane the Temple or cause a riot, he was kept prisoner for two years (A.D. 58–60) at Caesarea and at least two years at Rome.

MALTA

And when they had been brought safely through, then we found out that the island was called Malta.

Acts 28:1–2

After a long period of drifting before a southeasterly tempest, Paul's ship was finally wrecked on the island of Melita (now Malta). Everyone on board was saved, although the ship itself was a total loss (Acts 27:41–44). The traditional place where the passengers came ashore is the so-called Paul's Creek (see view above). Malta is the largest of five islands at the eastern end of the strait between Sicily and Tunis. It has been inhabited since prehistoric times, but the first settlers of whom we have historical information were the Phoenicians of Carthage. Their Semitic language, a dialect of Phoenician, is still spoken on the island and was also written in ancient times. Evidence of the mixed culture of ancient Melita, which became part of the Roman Empire after the Punic Wars, is provided by the bilingual inscription on the base of a dedicatory obelisk found there. The "barbaric" character of the people of Malta refers to their language and culture, which were non-Hellenic and therefore barbaric in the eyes of civilized people of Paul's time, but by no means to their manners, which are attested here to have been surprisingly kind.

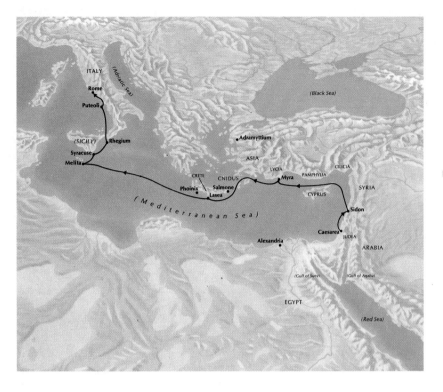

PAUL'S JOURNEY TO ROME

And when it was decided that we should sail for Italy, they proceeded to deliver Paul and some other prisoners to a centurion of the Augustan cohort named Julius.

. . . And there the centurion found an Alexandrian ship sailing for Italy

<small>ACTS 27:1, 6</small>

The centurion under whose charge the apostle Paul was taken to Rome, following his appeal for a trial before Caesar, was a member of the "Augustan" cohort. The name of this unit recalls the Emperor Caesar Augustus (LK. 2:1), who gave Rome peace after a century of civil wars. He firmly established his rule by means of his command of the Roman army. In the autumn of A.D. 60, Paul, accompanied once again by Luke, was sent to Rome in a ship. After stopping at several points along the Syrian coast and the southern shore of Asia Minor, the vessel was blown off course near Crete and wrecked upon the rocky coast of Malta (Melita) (ACTS 27–28:1). Paul was forced to spend the winter, sustained by the kindness of the primitive people, many of whom were miraculously healed (ACTS 28:2–10). Embarking again on a different ship, Paul proceeded toward Rome, stopping at Rhegium and landing at Puteoli on the Bay of Naples (ACTS 28:11–13). From there he and his party journeyed overland, traveling the last miles in the company of a delegation from the church at Rome that had come to greet them. For the next two years Paul lived in Rome under house arrest. According to I and II Timothy and Titus, he went again on missionary journeys before being once more imprisoned in Rome, where he is believed to have been beheaded in A.D. 66—one of the Christians Nero put to death.

FORUM OF TRAJAN

The dead bodies lying in the "streets" of the great city obviously refer to a disaster which is to overtake the city of Rome. Instead of the usual word for street, the Greek original reads *plateia*, meaning "broad street." At the time when Revelation was written, the imperial city had begun to be transformed by the building activities of successive emperors. In particular, the area north of the old Roman Forum had been developed by a series of new forums, beginning with that of Julius Caesar in which stood the temple of Venus Genetrix, the legendary ancestress of the Julian family. Then Augustus built another forum with the Temple of Mars the Avenger (of the assassination of Julius Caesar); Vespasian built a third with the temple of Peace; and Nerva added a fourth, small forum of Trajan, with its large semicircular wings (see illustration above). The building and town-planning activities which changed the face of imperial Rome justified the title of "the Great City" given it in this verse (Rev. 11:8).

And their dead bodies will lie in the street of the great city   Revelation 11:8

ROME IN THE TIME OF PAUL

*Rome was founded in the 8th century
B.C. atop the Palatine Hill, beside the
Tiber. As the city grew, a castle was
built on the nearby Capitoline Hill. By
the time of the founding of the Roman
Empire (31 B.C.), five other hills—the
Aventine, Caelian, Esquiline, Viminal,
and Quirinal—were included within the
city limits (see map). Although Rome
later grew much larger (and took in
several more hills), it retained its
traditional epithet: the "City of the
Seven Hills."*

*The four Gospels, which give an
account of the life and teachings of
Jesus, are followed by The Acts of the
Apostles, continuing the story of the
early days of Christianity up to Paul's
arrival in Rome. The Book of Acts is
followed by twenty-one epistles. Each
epistle is a theological message to a
Christian community or to all
Christians in the time of Paul or in the
first several decades after his death.
The Epistle to the Romans was written
by Paul, probably in Corinth about
A.D. 56. The illustration, showing
Romans 8:15–25, is from a third-
century compilation of Paul's epistles.*

*. . . to all who are beloved
of God in Rome, called as
saints: Grace to you and
peace from God our Father
and the Lord Jesus Christ*

ROMANS 1:7

81

SMYRNA

The Smyrna which is mentioned as the second of the seven churches of Asia was the city refounded (near the ruins of an earlier Ionian colony) in the fourth century B.C. Its geographical position at the head of a deep bay ensured its commercial prosperity; loyal to Rome, it flourished under imperial rule and vied with Ephesus and Pergamon for the primacy of the province. It was allowed first to erect a Temple to Tiberius, Livia and the Senate and thus obtained the title of "Warden of the Temple." The Jewish community in Smyrna seems to have existed since Hellenistic times; numerous inscriptions attest its importance and wealth into the third century. It seems to have given special trouble to the Christians living in the town, and was singled out for blame at the end of the message here. The photograph shows the present harbour and city of Smyrna, looking north.

"And to the angel of the church in Smyrna write. . . .

REVELATION 2:8

And I turned to see the voice that was speaking to me. And having turned I saw seven golden lampstands.

REVELATION 1:12

Troas
Adramyttium
Assos
PERGAMOS
THYATIRA
SARDIS
SMYRNA
PHILADELPHIA
EPHESUS
LAODICEA

(Aegean Sea)

Roman Roads —————

THE SEVEN CHURCHES (CITIES) OF ASIA

The Book of Revelation, written about ninety years after the birth of Christ, is a message of hope and encouragement addressed to the churches at a time when the Emperor Domitian's persecution of Jews and Christians alike was at its height. Although the seven-branched lampstands had become the recognized symbol of Judaism, the "golden lampstands" in the verse above represent the light of God as manifested in the Christian churches. The 4th century A.D. gold glass (left), discovered at Rome, shows two seven-branched lampstands surrounded by other Jewish ritual objects.

83

MAJOR BIBLICAL SITES
IN THE HOLY LAND

All locations are denoted by coordinates; these are ranged on the map with a horizontal scale from "A" through "K" and a vertical scale from "1" through "12." For example: The site of ABDON has the coordinates "F-3." At the top of the locator map the reader will see the letter "F" and trace an imaginary line down the page to a point even with the number "3" on the left side of the map. ABDON is in this area.

In those cases where a name pertains to more than one location, that name is followed by boldface numerals. For example: AROER **1**. . .**2**. If a boldface numeral is missing for a certain name—as in APHEK **2**. . .**3**—the missing location will be found by consulting the same entry in the Map Index on page 109.

A question mark following the name of a site or other geographic area on the map indicates that there is disagreement among scholars as to its exact location.

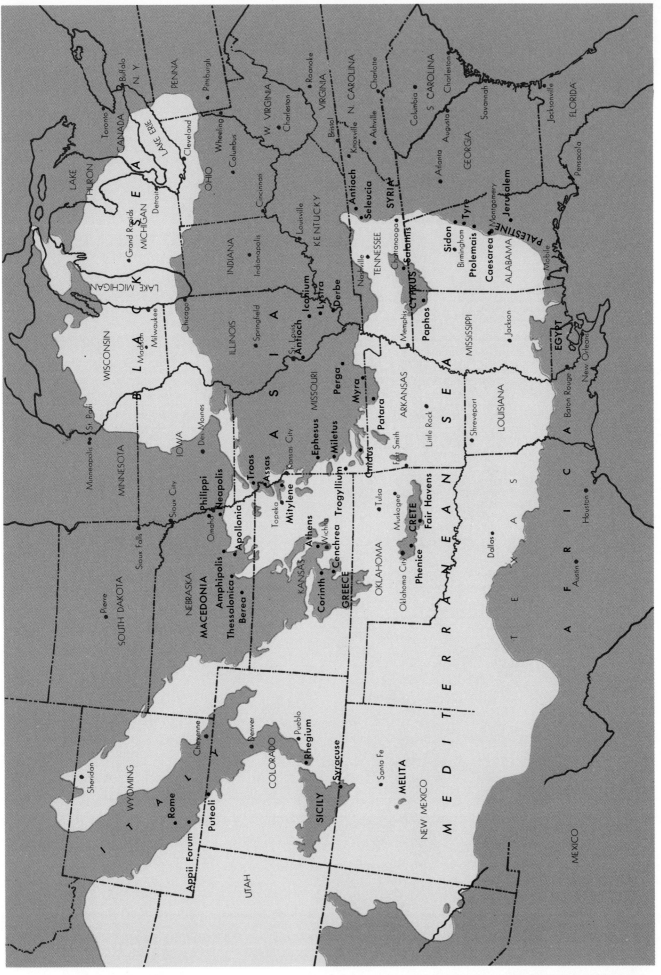

RELATIVE SCALE MAP

The Land and People
of the Bible

A landscape southwest of Jerusalem; from north to south, the 120-mile-long Holy Land, separating the Mediterranean from desert lands, is *ribbed by alternations of hills and valleys. There are, however, four main geographic regions, as shown on the map on page 71: the Mediterranean* *coastal region, the western hills, the fertile Jordan Valley, and the Transjordan plateau.*

The geography of the Bible is concerned with all those lands prominently mentioned in Scripture. This article will in general confine itself to the land and people of Palestine, for the biblical drama of God's redemptive activity is presented on that stage and is associated with those participants. Yet the lands and peoples of a given area are also inseparably bound together with the larger context of geography and history in which they are set. This is particularly true of Palestine, for it was located as a bridge between continents and as a crossroad for nations. This survey will necessarily be concerned with Egypt, Mesopotamia, Asia Minor, Greece, and Rome, Palestine's most immediate and influential neighbors.

The Land of Palestine

1. The Name Palestine

At a number of places in the KJV (Ex. 15:14; Is. 14:29-31; Joel 3:4) appears the territorial designation Palestine or Palestina. In the NASB the same place is always rendered more correctly Philistia. Indeed, the biblical term "Palestine" originally signified only the land of the Philistines, ancient enemies of

The Jordan River is approximately 700 feet below sea level and as it enters the Dead Sea it is 1,300 feet below sea level. Though the distance on a direct line between the Sea of Galilee and the Dead Sea is only 65 miles, the Jordan bends and curves to a length of more than 200 miles.

Israel. Rather early, however, Herodotus referred to the entire coastal area between Mount Carmel and Gaza as Palestinian Syria, or simply Palestine, and this meaning was then adopted by other Greek and Roman writers. Following the Jewish revolt of A.D. 132-135, the Romans applied the name "Palestine" to their province of Judaea, which extended inland beyond the River Jordan and the Dead Sea. That portion of this territory which lies west of the river and the sea was usually called Canaan by the ancient Hebrews (GEN. 11:31; 17:8; et al.), but at times after the conquest it was also referred to as the land of Israel (I SAM. 13:19), the land of the Lord (HOS. 9:3) and the holy land (ZECH. 2:12). In the New Testament it is spoken of as the land of promise (HEB. 11:9). In the Middle Ages the Church displayed a particular fondness for the terms "Holy Land" and "Promised Land."

2. Boundaries

In the course of its history Palestine has been a place of varying size. In general, the biblical reader understands the land involved as that which was promised to the patriarchs (GEN. 12:7; 13:15; 17:8; Ex. 6:8; et al.) and within which the Israelites settled according to the tribal distribution outline in Joshua, chapters 13 to 19. Thus understood, Palestine is the southern third of ancient Syria. Its geographical bounds are the Mediterranean Sea in the west, the great desert of Syria and Arabia in the east, the lower border of Lebanon in the north, and the southern extremity of the Dead Sea in the south. Including the land of the Philistines, but not that extending south to the Gulf of Aqabah as in the

89

British mandate of 1923-48, it covers an area of 10,150 square miles, approximately the size of the State of Maryland. According to United Nations figures from 1947, the population of this region numbered 1,851,000, about the same as that of Arkansas, but only one fifth that of Massachusetts, an area one sixth smaller in size. On the basis of biblical references, secular documents, and numerous ruins of former communities, it can be fairly assumed that the area was formerly more populous.

3. Geology

The underlying rock structure of the land of Palestine consists mainly of horizontal marine deposits of lime and chalk from the Jurassic and Cretaceous periods. The Jura is now visible in only a few places on the sides of the Jordan rift. Immediately above that, from the Early Cretaceous, and also appearing only in the Jordan rift and along the east coast of the Dead Sea, is a dark reddish-brown formation called Nubian sandstone. Above this lies the formations of the Later or Upper Cretaceous, named Cenomanian, Turonian, and Senonian, constituting the main part of the mountains of Palestine. The Cenomanian, a hard crystalline limestone, averages approximately 2,000 feet in depth and is charac-

Tell Harashim is in the area allotted by Joshua to the tribe of Naphtali. A recent excavation of this site has revealed pottery vessels and other objects that indicate the Israelites settled here at the time of the Conquest.

terized by canyon-like valleys formed from the runoff of rain. Above this and related to it is the Turonian. And on top of the Turonian is the Senonian, a delicate, dazzling white limestone averaging about 660 feet in thickness. Somewhat later a new phase of marine sedimentation developed the Tertiary stratum. The lowest level of this is called Eocene, a white or gray limestone found in the mountains of Palestine. The upper levels of the Tertiary period are known as Oligocene, Miocene, and Pliocene. Finally there was the Quaternary, or Pleistocene, period of marine sedimentation. These latter deposits constitute the present coastal plain as well as parts of the Jordan rift.

The horizontal rock deposits did not, however, remain undisturbed. After the Cretaceous period folding and warping of that strata occurred, particularly on the eastern side of the Judaean and Samaritan mountains and in present Transjordan. Between the Miocene and Pliocene periods, hence near the end of the Tertiary, the horizontal strata underwent an even more violent rending from north to south, resulting in the Jordan rift. Another north and south breach took place on the western edge of the west Jordan range. Later still southeast to northwest land ruptures developed, the most significant of which formed the Plain of Jezreel. Volcanic eruptions began in the mid-Pliocene age following the formation of the Jordan rift. They centered in what is now northern Transjordan and from there spread a mass of lava over the Jordan rift north and south of the Sea of Galilee. Accordingly, the entire southern part of the Galilean mountains is still overspread by a layer of basalt.

4. Topography

The relief features of Palestine are determined by the Jordan rift and its continuation north and south. This immense split in the mainland, resulting from the aforementioned geological fault, formed highlands west and east.

West of the Jordan, in what is termed Cisjordan, these highlands consist of the mountains of Judah, Samaria, and Galilee (JOSH. 20:7). The Judaean range includes the mountains of Hebron, which about 3 miles north of Hebron rise as high as 3,373 feet, and the mountains of Jerusalem, whose highest elevations are modern Mount Scopus and the Mount of Olives (II SAM. 15:30; EZEK. 11:23; MARK 13:3), rising 2,693 and 2,600 feet respectively. On the western side the Judaean hills are bordered by the so-called "Artuf fault," beyond which a sunken plateau forms rolling foothills 1,000 to 1,300 feet high. The eastern slope of the Judaean hill country lies in what is termed the "rain shadow"; hence, it is extremely low in rainfall and therefore a desert.

The Samaritan hill country begins at the northern edge of the mountains of Jerusalem and extends northwesterly to Mount Carmel (I KIN. 18:19; et al.) and northeasterly to Mount Gilboa (I SAM. 31:1-6), which in order have elevations of 1,736 and 1,737 feet. The highest elevations, however, are at the ancient city of Baal-Hazor (II SAM. 13:23), now called Tell Asur; Mount Ebal (DEUT. 11:29; 27:13); and Mount Gerezim (DEUT. 27:12; JOSH. 8:33), rising respectively to 3,333 and 3,085 and 2,890 feet. Since these Samaritan hills do not lie in the "rain shadow" and possess a gentle contour, they are more fertile and habitable than the Judaean ones.

The Galilean range commences north of the great inland Plain of Jezreel (JOSH. 17:16; JUDG. 6:33), called also Esdraelon, and falls into two natural parts, lower and upper Galilee. Lower Galilee consists of several east to west mountain ranges of moderate height. With adequate rainfall and an overall land structure similar to that of the Samaritan hill country, this area naturally lends itself to agriculture and a settled life. Its most notable mountain is Tabor (JUDG. 4:14; et al.), with an elevation of 1,850 feet. The upper Galilean mountains begin their rise, quite abruptly, just above the longitudinal line marking the northern end of the Sea of Galilee and reach their peak at Mount Jermaq, 3,963 feet, easily the highest elevation west of the Jordan. From there highlands of 2,300 to 2,600 feet continue north until they finally terminate at the valley of the River Litani, the natural boundary between Palestine and Syria. Beyond the river lies the rugged, well-watered, and biblically significant

The village of Shunem is seen in the foreground of this photograph, with the Gilboa mountain range in the distance across the Plain of Jezreel.

mountains of Lebanon (JOSH. 13:6; I KIN. 5:6; EZRA 3:7; PS. 29:5; ISA. 14:8), which rise to heights of approximately 6,000 feet.

Between the mountains of Western Palestine and the Mediterranean Sea lie a series of coastal plains formed by the late sedimentation already mentioned. North of the Carmel range is located the relatively small Plain of Accho, named after the ancient city situated in its midst. This plain extends northward to the promontory of Naqurah and eastward to the slopes of the Galilean hill country, but measures just 5 miles in width at its center. Flowing northwesterly through it to the sea is the River Kishon (JUDG. 4:13-16), now known as Nahr el Muqatta), which drains the whole Plain of Jezreel. A shallow bay, some 10 miles long, is formed between Accho and the foot of Carmel, creating a natural harbor on which is located the currently significant port city of Haifa. South of Carmel is the great plain generally known as the Palestinian Coastal Plain. In the Old Testament its northern part is referred to as Sharon (Is. 35:2) and is celebrated for its beauty and fertility. The whole plain extends southward to the Sinai Desert and eastward to the mountains of Judah and Samaria. Its greatest west to east expanse is at the southwest corner of the Judaean range, where it extends about 25 miles from Beersheba to the sea. Farther north it narrows down to 20 miles in width at Joppa, 7 miles at Caesarea, and less than 2 miles west of Carmel. Numerous small rivers and streams flow through it to the sea; hence the area is very productive. Along the seacoast are almost unbroken dune formations.

The highland formed east of the Jordan rift—that is, Transjordan—has the character of a plateau and indeed is an extension of the great Syro-Arabian Desert tableland still further to the east. It is marked by many small gullies and several great ravines that fall sharply into the Jordan Valley and the Dead Sea. Between the Brook Zered (DEUT. 2:14), now called Wadi Hesa, to the south and the Arnon (NUM. 21:13; JOSH. 13:16), presently known as Wadi Mojib, to the north, both of which empty into the Dead Sea, lies the land which was the principal territory of the Moabites.

The area extending from the Arnon northward and approaching the River Jabbok (DEUT.

3:16; cf. GEN. 32:22), now referred to as Nahr Zerqa, is known in Old Testament Hebrew as Mishor, the tableland (DEUT. 3:10). Its highest elevations, at Mount Nebo (DEUT. 32:49) and in the peaks just south of the Jabbok, rising to 3,760 and 3,590 feet, offer extensive views of the Jordan Valley and the mountains beyond to the west. Further east was the land of Ammon. Rabbathammon, the ancient city and strong fortress of the Ammonites, is modern Ammon, the capital of the present kingdom of Jordan. Beyond the Jabbok and continuing north to the River Yarmuk lies the region generally referred to in the Old Testament as the land of Gilead (JUDG. 11:4; ff.; et al.). Such a demarcation is not entirely precise, however, for even today many places south of the Jabbok bear the name, most notable Mount Gilead. In any case, the area between the two rivers is one of the loveliest and most richly forested in all of Palestine; very early in biblical times it was well known for the valuable gum from its trees called the ''balm of Gilead'' (GEN. 37:25; JER. 8:22). Its highest elevation is Mount Ajlun, 4,138 feet at its peak. Presently the entire region of Gilead is called Ajlun.

Across the Yarmuk to the north is an area composed of a number of extinct volcanic craters, now named the Jolan, probably after the ancient city of Golan (JOSH. 20:8), which extends to Palestine's northeastern boundary near the ancient city of Dan (JUDG. 18:29, et al.) and the foothills of Mount Hermon (DEUT. 3:8). Northwest of the Yarmuk lies a large fertile region, with an altitude of 1,600 to 2,100 feet, now referred to as en-Nuqreh. In the Old Testament both these places are probably included in the name ''Bashan,'' meaning ''plain'' (NUM. 21:33; ISA. 2:13; et al.). Two great lava formations are located east of the Lejah, Hellenistic Trachonitis; and the impressive snow-capped mountain called Hauran, probably biblical Bashan (PS. 68:15), rising to 6,036 feet. Directly north is Damascus (GEN. 14:15; ACTS 9:2 ff.), the celebrated capital city of ancient and modern Syria.

The Jordan rift itself extends from North Syria to the Gulf of Aqabah. In the center of this rift is the River Jordan, named ''the great river'' in Arabic. Its main sources are in a series of springs

Moses ordered the tribes of Israel to stand on the two peaks, Mount Gerizim and Mount Ebal (below), that rise on either side of Shechem, and solemnize their acceptance of God's commandments with a blessing and a curse (warning against sins). This marked the choice of Israel as the people of God (DEUT. 27:9). Mount Gerizim, seen at the left, is the more fertile of the two; it has numerous springs at its base. The choice of these mountains for this great gathering may have been suggested by the visits of Abraham and Jacob to Shechem centuries before (GEN. 12:6–7; 33:18–19).

The dry streambeds of the wastelands, such as this Negev watercourse. The streambeds are parched most of the time but can turn into roaring rivers of destruction, sweeping away persons who are foolish enough to camp close to their banks.

and small streams at the foot of Mount Hermon, near Dan and Caesarea Philippi (MARK 8:27), formerly Paneas, now Baniyas. From there it flows south through the well-watered and fertile area between the upper parts of Galilee and Bashan now called the Hulch Valley, probably the biblical Valley of Mizpah (JOSH. 11:3 ff.), which presently lies largely in modern Lebanon. Lake Hulch, about 4 miles long, was once located in the southern part of the valley, but it has now been drained by an artificial deepening of the Jordan outlet east of the very old city of Hazor (JOSH. 11:10).

Immediately south of Hulch the river descends, suddenly from 210 feet above to 630 feet below sea level in just 10 miles, to the Sea of Galilee, variously termed Chinnereth, Gennesaret, and Tiberias in the Bible (MARK 7:31; cf. NUM. 34:11; LUKE 5:1; JOHN 6:1). It measures 11 miles in length, 7 miles in width at its broadest, and 160 feet in depth. The waters of the lake are dark blue and drinkable, and abound in fish. Normally they are quite placid, yet sudden and violent storms of the kind frequently mentioned in the New Testament (MATT. 8:24; et al.) are not uncommon. Characterized by scenic mountains and fertile valleys, and possessing an agreeably warm climate, this lake region has been, and remains, one of the most popular and densely inhabited in the country. Around the shore were the very ancient and later cities of Chinnereth, Hammath, Capernaum, Tiberias, Bethsaida, and, perhaps, the unknown location of Cana.

From the southern end of the Sea of Galilee to the northern end of the Dead Sea, a distance of approximately 70 miles, the Jordan River cuts a deep, winding, unnavigable course through that section of the great rift which is the Jordan Valley proper, now known as el-Ghor; meaning "the lowland." At the river's edge is an even lower section of ground, in effect a sunken channel through the Ghor extending up to 1 mile in width, called the Zor, with dense jungle-like vegetation (Jer. 49:19). West and east of the valley are the Cisjordan highlands and the Transjordan mountain plateau. Only one major perennial stream comes down from the west; namely, the River Jalud, which enters the Jordan through the Bethshan Valley, a continuation of the Plain of Jezreel. This broad, level valley has a number of oases and was densely settled in the Canaanite and Israelite periods. It was the location of ancient Beth-shan (Josh. 17:11; Isa. 31:10), very near modern Beisan. Rather more affluents enter the Jordan from the great plateau to the east, the most notable of which are the Yarmuk and the Jabbok. Consequently, on this well-watered side of the valley in very early times were a chain of important communities, such as Zaphon and Succoth (Josh. 13:27), linked together by a road called "the way of the plain" (II Sam. 18:23). South of the Jabbok and continuing down to the Dead Sea the Ghor opens out into a desert plain more than 20 miles long and up to 12 miles wide. Some oases, fed by mountain springs, have been formed on both sides of the Jordan in the section; e.g., the highly significant one at Jericho (Josh. 6:1 ff.; et al.), perhaps Palestine's most ancient city. Opposite Jericho across the Jordan is that region of the desert plain called "the plains of Moab" (Num. 33:48).

The Jordan and the desert plain terminate at the Dead Sea. This inland body of water extends approximately 50 miles in length and 10 miles in breadth, and is divided into two parts by the Lisan peninsula. Its surface is 1,290 feet below sea level, and it reaches an interior depth of 1,300 feet in the northern part, the lowest point on earth. The saltiness of the water and the high temperature of the immediate surroundings prevent marine life in the lake or normal vegetation on its shores; hence the common term Dead Sea. It is also known in the Bible as the Salt Sea (e.g., Num. 34:3; Deut. 3:17), named thus for its character or location rather than effect. High cliffs and great canyons, entirely devoid of trees, rise abruptly on both sides of the sea, presenting wild and splendid scenery. In 1947 Bedouins discovered large jars containing scrolls in caves on the cliff at the northwest side, near the ruins of a community called Qumran, perhaps the biblical "city of Salt" (Josh. 15:62).

It should also be noted here that tradition places the ancient cities of Sodom, Gomorrah, Admah, and Zeboiim (Gen. 10:19) at the southern end of the Dead Sea. Some oases are located around the shores, particularly in the eastern gorges. On the western side is the important one at the old city of En-gedi (Josh. 15:62). Below the Dead Sea the Jordan rift continues between the mountains of the Negeb and Edom down to the Gulf of Aqabah, a distance of about 110 miles. This is the Arabah (Deut. 3:17), a desert expanse much coveted by Israel and her neighbors because of its wealth of copper ore and the important main road through it known as "the way to the Red Sea" (Num. 14:25, et al.). Opposite one another at the southern end of this highway and on the northern tip of the gulf were the strategic old port cities of Eloth and Ezion-geber (Deut. 2:8; I Kin. 9:26); the former is in modern Israel under the same name and the latter is now Aqabah in the present State of Jordan.

5. Climate

Palestine, together with the entire Mediterranean region, is situated in a zone of subtropical climate. It is therefore characterized by an alternation between a rainy season in the winter and a dry season in the summer, these being influenced in turn by the great sea to the west and the vast desert to the east. The rainy season normally begins in October or November and continues until April or May, with the heaviest falls usually occurring in January. Generally these rains are in the form of periodic heavy cloudbursts during a limited number of days rather than in steady showers extending over many days. Since geographic and associated climatic factors also influence precipitation, there are naturally great variations of rainfall in this small land of sharp physical contrasts. Only the coastal plains and the western half of the Cisjordan mountains receive an appreciable amount of rainfall, and the transition to arid regions east and south is extreme. For example, according to figures compiled for the decade from 1927 to 1936, the average annual rainfall was 20.7 inches at Haifa, 19.6 inches near Jaffa, 17 inches in Jerusalem, and just 15 inches in the western part of the Bethshan Valley. Inasmuch as rainfall is confined to a relatively small number of days in the rainy season, most of the streams in Palestine are intermittent, particularly those flowing into the Mediterranean. The Bible frequently refers to waters, called wadis, that are torrential on wet days but vanish rapidly in dry periods (JOB 6:15-20). Numerous natural springs offer some compensation, however, especially in the north, and even in biblical times man-made cisterns were employed to conserve water (II SAM. 3:26; JOHN 4:6). It is also noteworthy that all the perennial streams of Palestine except the Jordan are, according to the terrain, of necessarily short course.

Dew is an important precipitation element in all parts of Palestine. It alone supports even meager vegetation in the desert areas and also furnishes moisture in other areas during the summer dry season. Snow, on the other hand, falls very infrequently, and then only in the hills of Samaria and Judah.

Temperatures in Palestine are likewise subject to great fluctuations according to the season and location. Normally January is the coldest month and August the warmest. In the period between 1927 and 1936 the average January temperature was 12°C. on the coastal plain near Jaffa, and 8.2°C. in Jerusalem; the mean August temperature for the same decade was respectively 26°C. and 22°C. In the southern part of the Jordan Valley, in the vicinity of Jericho, temperatures are even higher in the warm season, ranging to 45°C.

It must also be noted that winds have a decided climatic effect on Palestine. Westerly winds normally prevail; they arise around noon, bringing with them not only the necessary rains of winter but also the cooling and refreshing summer breezes from the sea. Prominent easterly winds off the desert have an opposite effect, carrying into the land oppressive sultriness in the summer and cool but dry elements in the winter. In late spring and early fall the east wind is called "sirocco," and with its arrival the blossoming landscape quickly dries up and turns desolate.

Cedars of Lebanon are among the Near East's largest and most imposing trees. In ancient times the tops of the Lebanese mountains were covered by extensive cedar forests, of which only a few survive in modern times. This photograph was taken near Besharre at the source of the river Kadisha.

6. Vegetation

The flora of Palestine is naturally influenced by the fact that the country is located in a subtropical zone and by the sharp variations of altitude, rainfall, and temperature in different parts of the land. Although the Palestinian mountains were originally heavily forested, and continued partially so in Old Testament times (Josh. 17.14-18), in ancient days and until very recently they were periodically denuded by military invaders, economic necessity, or sheer neglect. True forests now exist only on the Carmel ridge and in former Gilead. The most notable forest trees are oak, terebinth, pine, and carob. Cedars continue to flourish in Lebanon. Steppe and desert growth consists of tamarisk, broom, and the so-called Christ's thorn, from which Christ's crown of thorns is legendarily said to have been made. The products of the land are basically as of old, and primitive methods of cultivation are still widely used. Among the cultivated plants, the various types of grain are of primary significance, above all wheat, barley, and kajir. These are common throughout the country but are especially abundant in northern and southern Transjordan. The principal fruit trees are the olive, the fig, the pomegranate, the date palm, and the banana, as well as the grape vine.

7. Animals

The fauna of Palestine is unusually varied and substantially the same today as in biblical times. Among the wild animals, predatory creatures such as wolves, jackals, hyenas, foxes, and wild dogs are still prominent. On the other hand, the lion (Jer. 49:19) and the bear (Isa. 11:7) have become extinct, except that the latter is still found in the Lebanon range. Game animals include gazelles, rabbits, and groundhogs, as well as wild boars in the dense tropical vegetation along the Jordan and droves of wild goats in the deserts of Judah. There are still some roebuck deer (I Kin. 4:23) in central Transjordan. Other species such as the red deer and the antelope, however, appear to have died out altogether. Numerous kinds of predatory birds, such as vultures, continue to feed on decaying flesh left in open fields, and the ostrich (Job 39:13), though nearly extinct, still inhabits certain desert sections. Snakes and lizards in great numbers and varieties abound everywhere in the land. Of the host of insects, the

Reproduced here is an Egyptian relief from the tomb of Mereruka at Sakkarah (Sixth Dynasty, 2350–2200 B.C.), showing men feeding rams and a train of fattened oxen.

Glass (or "crystal") was valued as an article of luxury, and was often used as a substitute for precious stones. At the left is a vessel of glass from about 400 B.C.

migratory locust was and is most notable. As recently as 1915 a great plague, like those alluded to in the Bible (Ex. 10:12-15; Joel 2; et al.), literally devastated all green plant life. Among the domesticated animals are donkeys, oxen, horses, and camels, used largely as creatures of burden, and chickens and pigeons for food purposes. Sheep and goats, which are found in flocks everywhere in the country, are now as always of great significance for the food, milk, and clothing material they provide.

8. Mineral Resources

Palestine is very deficient in mineral resources. Scripture does say, nevertheless, that it is "a land whose stones are iron, and out of whose hills you can dig copper" (Deut. 8:9). As for iron, however, only a few ancient mines have been discovered, and these are confined to a relatively small area around the Jabbok in central Transjordan. Of course, the text may have meant to include the Lebanon region, where there were numerous mines which belonged for a time to the kingdom of David. Even so, the supply and processing of iron were at best probably very limited (cf. 1 Sam. 13:19-22). There is evidence that copper was extensively mined and smelted in the Arabah from ancient Punon (Num. 33:42-43) south to the Gulf of Aqabah, which apparently was the source of Solomon's supply. On the other hand, Cisjordan is totally lacking in both iron and copper. Although the waters of the Dead Sea are unusually abundant in salt and other minerals, we have no clear indication that they were utilized in the biblical period. Gold and silver are often mentioned in the Bible, but had to be imported into the country, probably from southern Arabia (1 Kin. 10:21-25).

The Historical Geography of Palestine

1. Pre-Israelite Period

Numerous remnants of the various stages of the Stone Age, uncovered at scattered sites throughout the country, attest to human existence in Palestine in very ancient time. From the Old Stone Age there are characteristic flints and even skeletal remains. At this stage man dwelt on the land in caves and obtained his food solely by hunting and foraging. Already in the Middle Stone Age (c. 10000-6000 B.C.), however, Palestine had developed a discernible cultural form, called Natufian after the Wadi en-Natuf, where it was first identified. In the early part of this stage, while still living in caves and employing stone implements, man had learned to till the soil and, apparently, to domesticate animals. Somewhat later the first crude houses of packed mud began to appear. The Late Stone Age, known as Neolithic (c. 6000-4000 B.C.), and usually divided into prepottery and pottery phases, reveals further cultural development thousands of years before the Israelite period. This is particularly evident at the mound of Jericho and in the Yarmuk Valley. Rather well-developed stone tools and methods of cultivation, clay vessels and statues (perhaps to gods), and less crude dwellings of mud-brick, often in villages surrounded by strong stone walls, are characteristic of this stage.

The Copper-Stone Age, termed Chalcolithic (c. 4000-3000 B.C.), which witnesses to a marked cultural flowering everywhere in the ancient East, especially in Mesopotamia, is also visible in Palestine. Of particular importance is the Ghassulian culture, so named for Tuleilat el-Ghassul in the Jordan Valley, where it was first discovered. Stone implements were still employed in this age, but copper was also in use and the houses were more firmly made of brick and stone and were often richly decorated with painted frescoes. It should also be noted that people of this culture buried food with their dead, perhaps indicating an early belief in life after death.

Investigations into the Bronze Age (c. 3000-1200 B.C.) have resulted in the identification of a considerable number of Palestinian city settlements dating from the different phases of that time span. They are generally marked by massive fortifications, extensive drainage, and many fine homes. Among these communities are such later biblically significant places as Megiddo, Beth-shan, Ai, Shechem, and Gezer.

Additional information about these ancient cities of Palestine has been furnished by Egyptian documents from the Late Bronze Age, especially in the accounts of Pharaoh Thuthmosis III (c. 1490-1435 B.C.) and in those dealing with the reign of Amenhotep IV (c. 1370-1353 B.C.), known to us from the famous Amarna letters. They confirm that the land was then indeed divided into innumerable small city-states. They furthermore clearly indicate that these communities were largely under Egyptian domination for an extended time, although because of pressing internal affairs and open rebellion in Palestine, this power was substantially reduced in the so-called Amarna Period (c. 1400-1350 B.C.).

The aggressive foreign policy of Pharaohs Sethos I (c. 1309-1290 B.C.) and Rameses II (c. 1290-1224 B.C.), designed to re-establish Egyptian control throughout Asia, was at least successful in restoring a strong hold on the Late Bronze Age cities of Palestine. But that success did not endure long. Literature from the time speaks of continuing turmoil in the land and likewise distinguishes between established and bothersome nomadic peoples there.

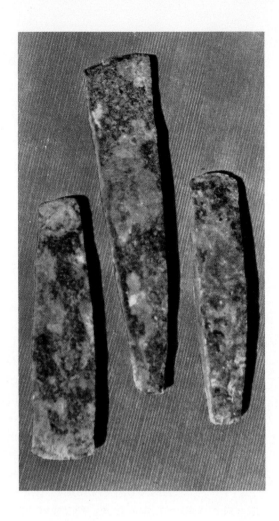

The illustration shows the earliest copper objects yet discovered in western Palestine, dating to the end of the fourth millennium B.C. The copper adzes were unearthed in 1956 at Metser, near the entrance to the Pass of Megiddo.

Together with such external evidence the Old Testment itself shows that the Israelites were not the first, or sole, inhabitants of the land of Palestine. Although the information there is uneven (GEN. 15:19-21; EX. 13:5; 23:23, 38; DEUT. 7:1; JOSH. 3:10), it clearly points to a great variety of indigenous elements in the land prior to the arrival of the tribes. Among these, Amorites, Canaanites, Hittites, Hurrians, and Philistines seem to have been the most important.

Amorites and Canaanites were apparently of common Semitic culture and probably represent successive waves of the same semi-nomadic penetration into Palestine from the end of the third millennium B.C. onward. Indeed, the two names are frequently used interchangeably in the Old Testament to designate a substantial portion of the land's residents at the time of Israel's entry.

The Hittites are a people of very obscure origin. It is now known, however, that they had a strong kingdom in Asia Minor (cf. Cappadocia) in the sixteenth century B.C. Racially an admixture, their language and leadership were essentially Indo-European. Hittites were apparently present in Palestine as early as the time of Abraham, and it is now believed that they had a decisive influence on the land and the whole people (EZEK. 16:3, 45). Horites are frequently mentioned in the Bible (e.g., GEN. 14:6; 36:20; DEUT. 2:12). Once regarded as cave dwellers, they are now widely understood as the Hurrians, as Indo-European directed people whose center was in northern Mesopotamia and one of whose communities was Nuzi. Laban's home was probably located in that region, and texts discovered at Nuzi are especially helpful in understanding many otherwise obscure Old Testament happenings, including aspects of the Laban-Jacob stories in Genesis, chapters 29-31. That the Hurrians were a significant people and prominently present in Palestine by the thirteenth century B.C. is attested by the fact that the Egyptians then called the land Huru. It should furthermore be noted that the name "Hivite" is now generally held to be a corrupt form of Horite.

The Philistines were part of the Sea Peoples who came from the eastern Mediterranean world. They entered Palestine at about the same time as the tribes of Israel (c. 1200 B.C.), following an unsuccessful attack on Egypt. They settled mainly in the coastal area known as Philistia but, bearing a strong military tradition and being skilled in the use of iron, particularly for weaponry, they soon occupied a larger portion of the land. Later they posed a constant threat to the Israelites, only being put down finally by David.

Other peoples connected with early Palestine in the Old Testament (Jebusites, Perizzites, Girgashites, etc.) are of uncertain ethnic nature. It has been suggested that they may have been subgroups within the Hittite and/or Hurrian races. However that may be, all such names other than Amorite and Canaanite, including those discussed above, represent non-Semitic elements in the population of Palestine prior to, or coincident with, the Israelite entry. In due course all these peoples, whatever their origin, adopted that style of cultural life which the Old Testament generally knows as Canaanite.

2. Israelite Era

The ancestors of the Israelites were also present in Palestine in the latter stages of the period just discussed. They are the biblical patriarchs. They arrived in the land in the late third and early second millennia B.C., as a small part of that great seminomadic Semitic penetration already mentioned. At first they roamed the country in strictly seminomadic fashion (GEN. 37:12 ff.), but judging from certain Egyptian sources, they apparently made a rapid transition to sedentary life, taking up agricultural pursuits and even in due course establishing towns and cities. While many of these Israelite forefathers went down into Egypt at various times during the mid-second millennium B.C., some doubtless remained in Palestine up to the time of Joshua.

Properly speaking, however, the Israelite era in Palestine begins with the biblically momentous occupation, or reoccupation, of the land which occurred about 1250 to 1200 B.C. Following the exodus from Egypt under Moses and the reception of a peculiar charter of faith at Sinai, the various Hebrew elements that were once represented in Palestine entered the land again, and in force, as the united people Israel. Whether this occupation took place suddenly and completely, as reported in Joshua, chapters 1-12, or rather slowly and partially over an extended time, as presented in Judges 1:16-31 (I KIN. 9:20 f.), cannot be argued here. It is sufficient to say, on the basis of broad biblical tradition supported by substantial archaeological evidence, that this new people Israel violently and decisively took the land of Palestine in the thirteenth century B.C.

On the other hand, Israel's taking of the land did not mean immediate union of Palestine into a uniform political system. At first the country was divided into twelve tribal areas in confederation. The geographical extent of these regions is rather precisely stated in Joshua, chapters 13-19, and can be generally visualized by consulting a standard map dealing with the subject. Such boundaries are not always clear, however, as is shown, for example, in Simeon's allotment of "an inheritance in the midst of" Judah (JOSH. 19:9). Furthermore, certain of these tribal holdings have to be understood as reflecting theoretical or subsequent situations, for some of the apportioned land in fact remained outside Israelite control well into the period of the Judges and even until the time of the monarchy. Of decisive significance for the geography, economy, and history of Israel is the fact that, whereas the inhabitants were in former times clustered in and around the fertile valleys, now the population was largely scattered across the land.

The tribal confederacy endured about 200 years. Thereafter, as a result of mounting Philistine aggression and the necessity of concerted response to it, the tribes formed themselves into an essentially united monarchy, first under Saul (c. 1020-1000? B.C.) and then, more importantly, under David (c. 1000-961 B.C.). The latter established Jerusalem as a strong national capital, expanded Israel's realm to its maximum limits, and elevated the country to the status of a major world power.

Besides the effect it had in the assault on Jericho, the Israelite din of horn blasts and shouts served in other battles to create confusion and panic in the ranks of their foes (see JUDG. 7). A similar description of the use of rams' horns as trumpets occurs in one of the Dead Sea Scrolls found at Qumran. Pictured here is the passage, written in Hebrew: "The priests shall blow on the six trumpets of assault a high-pitched intermittent note to direct the fighting, and the Levites and all the band of horn-blowers shall blow in unison a great battle fanfare to melt the heart of the enemy." The horn-blowing figure is from a 900 B.C. relief from Carchemish, the capital city of the Hittites, a powerful people who lived to the north of Canaan.

Nevertheless, as the Bible well shows, it was Solomon (c. 961-922 B.C.) who brought Israel into an age of unparalleled military security, economic prosperity, and cultural activity. While Saul and David reigned more or less within the old tribal structure, Solomon, in order to facilitate tax collection, reorganized the land into twelve administrative districts in marked disregard of the former names and boundaries. Notable is the impression that the reorganization involved only the northern realm, perhaps implying that Israel and Judah already had the character of separate and independent units (1 KIN. 4:7-19). After the death of Solomon, and largely because of his oppressive policies, the monarchy indeed split into two kingdoms, Judah and Israel. Although there were intermittent periods of peace and achievement throughout the land, the history of the two realms in the following 350 years is one of rivalry, warfare, dissipation, and, finally, loss of identity for both.

The boundary between Judah and Israel was vigorously disputed for generations (e.g., 1 KIN. 14:30) and fluctuated according to their relative power. Virtual civil war caused by this and other issues between them so weakened both that they were unable to maintain control over the vast areas conquered under the united monarchy. Theoretically, Transjordan belonged to Israel, but it was effectively held only in times of Syrian weakness and through the particularly energetic efforts of leaders such as Ahab (869-850 B.C.) and Jeroboam II (786-746 B.C.). Between 734 and 733 B.C. all Israelite holdings in Galilee and Transjordan were substantially lost to Assyria, and in 721 B.C., following the conquest of Samaria by Sargon II (722-705 B.C.), the remainder of the northern kingdom became an Assyrian province. In accordance with the conqueror's policy, many Israelites were deported (II KIN. 17:24) and the land was resettled with peoples banished from elsewhere. Israel was finished as an independent political entity. Judah, on the other hand, barely escaped the same fate in 701 B.C. when, while systematically destroying its cities and carrying off its people, the forces of Sennacherib (705-681 B.C.) were suddenly recalled to handle an urgent problem at home. Following the subsequent collapse of the Assyrian Empire, Judah's situation markedly improved, at least

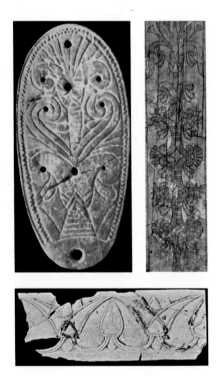

Solomon's Temple consisted of three parts: the vestibule, the nave, and the inner sanctuary. Excavations have revealed the remains of Canaanite temples with the same plan. One such temple is shown below (15th or 14th century B.C.). It also had three divisions, and in the inner sanctuary (seen in the foreground) ritual implements were discovered. The "boards of cedar" lining the Temple were ornamented with carvings (I KIN. 6:18).

temporarily. Capitalizing on the political vacuum in Palestine, Josiah (640-609 B.C.) took control of a large portion of Israel's former territory, put through a sweeping reform (II KIN. 22:3-23:25), and thereby restored a measure of national unity and prosperity in the land. In 609 B.C., however, Josiah was defeated and killed at Megiddo by the Egyptian forces under Neco II (609-593 B.C.). Thereafter Judah existed only as a vassal, first of Egypt and then of Babylon, the new great power in the East. Repeated rebellion in Judah against this subjugation provoked Babylon to even more drastic steps: in 598 B.C. Jehoiachin and numerous leading citizens were deported, and in 587 B.C. the troops of Nebuchadnezzar burned Jerusalem and utterly decimated Judah. By the middle of the sixth century B.C. Persia, under Cyrus (550-530 B.C.), was the dominant power in the East. Babylon fell to it in 539 B.C., and with this Palestine probably passed automatically to Persian control. In the first year of his rule in Babylon, however, Cyrus decreed the political and religious restoration of Judah in Palestine (EZEK. 1:2-4; 6:3-5). Accordingly, though with a somewhat diminished area, Judah was granted the status of a Persian province under a native governor, and the exiles, who regarded themselves as the true remnant of Israel, were allowed to return to their land. We know very little about the political division of Palestine in this period. From what information we do have, it appears that four other provinces surrounded Judah, namely, Ammon in the east, Idumaea in the south, Ashdod in the west, and Samaria in the north (cf. NEH. 4:1 f.). Samaria, inhabited by residual Israelites and those peoples resettled there under the Assyrians, became the center of open and veiled resistance to the new "Jewish" community in Judah. After about 200 years the vast Persian Empire, including Palestine, was in turn taken over by Alexander the Great (336-323 B.C.). He sought not only the liberation of Greeks from Persian bondage but also the thorough Hellenization of the Orient. On the basis of limited information, it does not appear that the political and administrative structure of Palestine was altered during Alexander's short reign. Following his death, the land became a place of contention between two rival Hellen-powers, the Ptolemies in Egypt and the Seleucids in Syria, until the issue was finally settled by the victory of Antiochus III (223-187 B.C.) at ancient Paneas in 198 B.C. Under the Seleucids Palestine apparently belonged to the larger political area, or satrapy, called Coele Syria and Phoenecia and remained separated into numerous provincial regions on the order of the former Persian structure. In this period, however, the provinces of the land were further divided into smaller administrative units, known as toparchies.

Antiochus IV Epiphanes (175-163 B.C.) pursued a Hellenization policy which utterly threatened Jewish religion and life. It finally resulted in the so-called Maccabean Revolt, thus designated after the third son of a priestly family (later called Hasmonaean), named Judas, but nicknamed Maccabeus, meaning "the hammer." He and certain of his brothers, especially Simon, who thought of himself as both priest and king, gained control of the province of Judah and even extended its frontiers (cf. 1 Macc. 14:5) into Samaria and east of the Jordan. John Hyrcanus (135-104

Three excavated levels or terraces of Herod's palace on Masada and, in the valley, the remains of the Roman siegeworks (the long, thin line) and encampments (the square outlines). The illustration shows part of a mosaic floor in Herod's palace.

B.C.), son of Simon, and his successors expanded Judah's borders even further within these areas as well as into Idumaea and Galilee, with the end result that the Hasmonaean monarchy ultimately embraced the whole territory of the old Israelite tribes. The success of the new kingdom was short-lived. Taking full advantage of the collapse of the Seleucid state and the incompetence of the later Hasmonaean rulers, Pompey conquered Palestine for the Romans in 63 B.C. and thereupon annexed the land to the newly constituted province of Syria. As part of an extensive Roman reorganization, in which the land was divided into a system of vassal states and cities, the Hasmonaeans were denied the title of king and, apart from Galilee, Idumaea, and a strip of land east of the Jordan called Peraea, their conquered regions were liquidated.

3. New Testament Age

After considerable internal dispute and intrigue, Herod succeeded in having himself appointed king of Judah, or Judaea, by the Roman Senate in 40 B.C. Following a series of military campaigns to wrest his kingdom from the control of certain Jewish antagonists, he assumed his royal office in Jerusalem in the year 37 B.C. His realm ultimately included all land west of the Jordan as well as Gaulanitis, Batanaea, Trachonitis, Auranitis, and Peraea to the east, thus taking in virtually the whole of Palestine. Only the regions belonging to the free cities of the so-called Decapolis (MATT. 4:25; MARK 5:20; 7:31), established by Pompey, remained beyond his domain. After his death in 4 B.C., and probably in accord with the emperor's desire, the kingdom was divided among his three younger

A row of graceful columns lines the edge of the 3rd century A.D. marketplace in Gerasa, a city of Palestine in the time of Jesus. The columns originally supported a portico, or covered walkway, that was lined with shops, taverns, and other places of business.

sons. Archelaus, with the title "ethnarch," was given Judaea, Samaria, and Idumaea; Antipas received Galilee and Peraea, and Philip the territories of Batanaea, Auranitis, and Trachonitis (LUKE 3:1), both with the designation "tetrarch." But responding to widespread displeasure with despotic Herodian rule, particularly in the central and southern part of the land west of the Jordan, Augustus removed Archelaus from power in A.D. 6 and banished him to Gaul. Thereafter, Judaea, Samaria, and Idumaea became a Roman administrative district, composed of eleven toparchies, under a procurator, the best known of which was Pontius Pilate (A.D. 26-36). Under Herod's grandson, Agrippa I (A.D. 37-44), the old monarchy was somewhat restored. Through shrewd support of the emperors, Agrippa successively achieved control of Abilene (LUKE 3:1) and the tetrarchy of Philip in the year A.D. 37, Galilee in A.D. 39, and eventually Judaea, Samaria, and Idumaea in A.D. 40, so nearly the entire territory formerly ruled by his grandfather. Yet his kingdom was more a useful device of Caligula and Claudius than a real political entity and, indeed, was practically dissolved after his death in the year A.D. 44. Although his son, Agrippa II (A.D. 53-93), was allowed the title of king and was finally granted certain small consolation holdings in the north by Claudius and Nero, together with supervision of the Temple in Jerusalem, he was in effect denied his father's kingdom, and all of Palestine henceforth became a Roman province under procurators, the whole officially named Judaea.

Tensions between the Roman authorities and the population of the land naturally appeared almost from the beginning of occupation. Subsequent maladministration, religious interference, plundering of the land and even of the Temple, and brutal persecution of the people made matters progressively worse. Finally, between A.D. 66 and 70, with provocations on both sides, deep-seated hostility broke into violent insurrection. The rebels won a decisive early battle against Cestius and hence were in control throughout the land. Later, however, the mighty Roman legions, first under Vespasian and then Titus, swept through the country from the northwest and, after an epic siege and defense, took Jerusalem in the year A.D. 70, burned the Temple, and completely destroyed whatever remained of the city. This was the next to last stage in Israel's final political annihilation. Another great rising of rebellious Jews occurred under Hadrian (A.D. 117-138), led by a certain Simon bar Cochba (A.D. 132-135), perhaps the ben Koseba known from documents recently found near the Dead Sea. Even though this rebellion was likewise quite successful at the outset, bringing new independence to Israel, the Romans once more devastated the country. From this point the land became a complete Roman province. On the site of another destroyed Jerusalem was erected the Roman Colonia Aelia Capitolina. In all probability the land was henceforth referred to as Palestine, or Palestina, rather than Judaea.

This material is an adaptation from an article written by J. R. Hiles and based on standard works in the field.

INDEX OF ILLUSTRATIONS

MAP INDEX

INDEX TO SCRIPTURE QUOTATIONS

INDEX

In those cases where a name pertains to more than one location, that name is followed by boldface numerals.

For example: APHEK **1** . . . **2** . . . **3**. A question mark following the name of a site or other geographic area on a map indicates that there is disagreement among scholars as to its exact location.

NOTES

NOTES

NOTES

Acknowledgements

All scripture quotations are from the New American Standard Bible,
copyright by THE LOCKMAN FOUNDATION, La Habra, California and
used by permission.

The relative scale map: copyright 1944 by NATIONAL PUBLISHING COMPANY.
Used by permission.